Just

Everyday
Folks

Just

Everyday
Folks

An Adirondack Family
1925-1950

by L.R. Warner

Library of Congress Control Number:		2013910485
ISBN:	Hardcover	978-1-4836-5266-5
	Softcover	978-1-4836-5265-8
	Ebook	978-1-4836-5267-2

This book was printed in the United States of America.

Rev. date: 08/20/2013

To order additional copies of this book, contact:
Xlibris LLC
1-888-795-4274
www.Xlibris.com
Orders@Xlibris.com
134786

Dedicated to the memory of my parents,
Lee and Pearl (Farrington) Raymond,
and my brothers, Maxwell and Verne Raymond,
without whom there would be no story.

Acknowledgements

With thanks to Barbara, Caroline, Martha, Milda, and Vi for helping to spark my memory by their questions: "Do you remember . . . . ?" "Did you ever . . . . ?" and their confirmations: "I remember that !" or "We did the same thing!"

Contents

Preface

This novelette is based on a series of anecdotes written over a period of several years, plus others never before published. As moves fluctuated between the main places we called home, so the story also fluctuates as one memory leads to another. Although it is reminiscent of the rural life of everyone we knew, it is only a recount of the life of my family from one family member—me!

. . . and there will be clichés, those trite expressions that are frowned on in the literary world today. They are so appropriate in speaking of life as I remember it that I say *if the shoe fits, put it on!*

Forward

*W*arrensburg *News*, May 7, 1902: "Casey's Hotel, otherwise known as the Dew Drop Inn, located four miles north of North River on the road to Indian Lake, was destroyed by fire Tuesday night. The barn, opposite the hotel building on the other side of the road, also burned."

But the Dew Drop Inn, where I was born on May 23, 1925 to Lee and Pearl (Farrington) Raymond, joining my two brothers, Maxwell and Verne, still stands—its rebuilding unknown to me. Dad may have acquired the place, when the new State road went through in 1922 and it was found to be in the way of construction.

The location was within a couple miles of where his parent's, Emery and Rhoda (Cross) Raymond's, farm stood on Cleveland Road. The story was that the Inn was drawn to the other side of the road on skids by a single team of oxen on the ice in the wintertime. It was then placed on a half-acre of land purchased from Mr. and Mrs. Walter Janis.

Apparently, unable to resume the hotel business at the time, my parents took advantage of an opportunity to manage an already established country store trade. They kept the Inn for their home, but rented it out.

All of this took place before my birth, but it would be at the country store where my first memories began. We will hear much more about life at the store, the farm, and the Dew Drop Inn.

Christian Hill Settlement

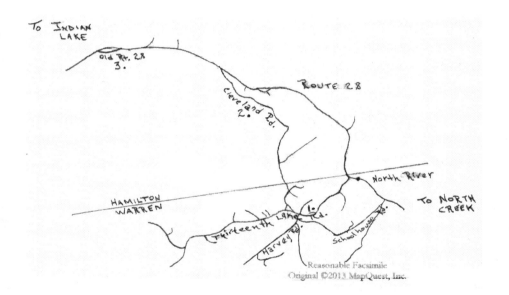

1. *Raymond's Store*
2. *Family Farm*
3. *Dew Drop Inn*

Farewell
To the Store

From a post card: courtesy, Frank Jay, Jr.

*T*he photograph shown of the store depicts a two-story building, rumored to actually be three about which I have no knowledge. I know there was a sizable attic. I can only speculate about the door over the porch roof. When we lived there, I was obviously too short to look up and notice it. I am sure it was barricaded by a piece of furniture inside. Trees and weeds growing up through the deteriorating foundation are all that remains of that building.

With the small population of the community nearly everyone was acquainted; therefore, the store was a big part of the social hub of the place. Local events, political views, and gossip were exchanged on the porch in moments of camaraderie before going inside.

Stepping over the threshold, one faced the tall, potbellied woodstove setting in the center of the room. An ornately designed, nickel-plated fixture resembling a crown topped the fire-pit belly, underneath of which was a matching metal ring. The beauty of the woodstove ended there as the eyes swept downward to the ash-pit, where streams of tobacco juice aimed at the draft door opening by old-timers setting around to spin their yarns had missed, leaving ugly stains and odors. The fire-safe pad the stove sat on was also stained. A live coal falling on still-wet tobacco juice often smoldered there.

Long counters on each side-wall and one, halfway across the back, displayed the merchandise. Beginning with the counter on the left, a long glass-case held tobacco products, including slabs of chewing tobacco about two inches by six inches in measurement. That case was kept locked to ensure

that my brothers and their buddies would not yield to the temptation to help themselves to the *forbidden fruit*. From the slab of dried, compressed tobacco leaves, Dad would cut a chunk per order of the customer. With every delivery of tobacco supplies,

Maxwell Raymond on bike. Verne Raymond standing at the Dew Drop Inn. Circa 1925

I became engaged to the salesman with the paper-band from the free cigar he gave to Dad. What a thrill it was when he gave me a real, sterling-silver baby ring with a tiny, garnet-stone inset on the day we left the store.

On one end of the counter center-opening stood the big, red, hand-operated coffee grinder; the pleasant aroma of freshly ground coffee beans permeated the air, offsetting the often offensive odor from the stove ash-pit. A cash register and a separate, small machine for tallying the day's sales were located on the other end of the center-opening.

Other items along that counter were the large, round, wooden box of store cheese and the scale that portions of the cheese were weighed on. The scale resembled a mantle-clock with a flat shelf on top. An oblong roll of heavy, white paper, on a stand with a cutting edge, sat next to the scale and a cone-shaped roll of twine was suspended from the ceiling. It

4

was amazing how quickly Dad could cut a wedge of cheese for a customer, weigh it, wrap it in a piece of that paper, and tie it together with a length of twine.

Behind the counter, on the floor, was a large crate made of slats, wired loosely together for air circulation, which held bread products. The supplier for these was Scott Severence—his name painted on the box.

Most of the wall space, over the counter on the opposite wall, was taken up by shelves displaying footwear. Ladies calf-high, white canvas-shoes with laces had such narrow, pointed toes I think they could have been a lethal weapon. A size larger than what most shoes needed to be must have been purchased to compensate for the extremely narrow toes. Men's over-the-ankle, black leather-shoes featured broad toes and hooks at the top, where shoelaces were secured in the same manner as lacing side to side through holes. I remember children's shoes only by a Buster Brown poster. Available for inclement weather were high, rubberized-cloth overshoes, fastened together by clasps. Men's ankle-high, rubber-shoes were fastened together likewise. Different sized shoe-lasts (iron pedestals about 18 inches high, on top of which was a shoe-shaped platform), packaged soles, and heel lifts for do-it-yourself repair sat on the counter underneath.

Men's white straw Panama-hats and stiff, detachable white shirt-collars were also displayed there. I don't think these fashionable items were much in demand since so many were left when my parents gave up the business. We kids used them for dress-up play for years.

Remaining space on that counter was filled with sewing notions. Company names on needle packets read: Coates and Clark, or in later years, J.A. Coates and Sons.

I know that canned foods were available as were various apothecary items, kept on high selves beyond my sight and reach, preschooler that I was. I do not remember candy, perhaps placed strategically for the same reason. Neither can I recall any food requiring refrigeration. But the store inventory did list round cardboard containers in quart- and pint-sizes for ice cream. These were brown in color and waxed inside. I still have a metal ice cream scoop from that era.

The half-counter on the back wall was cluttered with cartons, perhaps holding merchandise for restocking the shelves. At the end of it was a door leading to the kitchen, where one could ascend stairs to the second-floor bedrooms or exit onto the back porch.

Dad was never too busy to chat with or assist a customer. The big chain stores of the Twenty-first Century carry a huge assortment of modern household needs and wants, but gone is the one-on-one customer service, and it is just by chance for a person to meet a neighbor when shopping.

Although there are so-called country stores today (not to be confused with mini-marts), many of them function more as a nostalgic endeavor rather than being a single means of livelihood for a family.

*M*ore than likely, a country store was also the residence of the owner's family in the Good Old Days. So it was for my folks, when we lived on Thirteenth Lake Road, in the town of North River, New York, in the Adirondack Mountains. The settlement was known as Christian Hill. It probably came into existence as a result of what would become the world's largest industrial garnet supplier located there—Barton's Mines. The name may have evolved as several Protestant churches stood in close proximity of each other at the time.

My memories of life at the country store are sporadic, and limited mostly to things I witnessed rather than participated in. Under Mother's watchful eye I seldom got beyond the confines of the front stoop, but from that vantage point I came to know many people and some of their individualities. For nostalgia sake, and perhaps of some historical interest, I shall list a few names and bits of memorable trivia from a child's point of view.

Hugh and Hattie Roblee lived next door, below the store. My teenage brother, Verne, had such a crush on their teenage daughter, Geneva. Beyond the Roblees was the family of Rob Smith, with a little boy named Curtis; farther on lived Will Reed. The land above the store was undeveloped.

Across the road were the Rogers, Bennetts, Max and Mabel Burns, and their son, Jimmy—my same age. When his mother came to the store, he and I made mud pies in a sawdust pile while she shopped. Jimmy and I had chicken pox at the same time; I contracted whooping cough with it, but wasn't very ill. I do recall Mother giving me spoonfuls of melted chicken fat to ease the long, drawn-out whoops.

The Methodist Church was near the Burn's residence, where it still stands. At a community recreation hall on that side of the road, square dances were held every Saturday night. Occasionally, Mother served the hot dogs and beverages at intermission. Returning home one night after closing the kitchen, she found Dad asleep in bed and the bed mattress smoldering. He must have fallen asleep while smoking. She shook him awake and both of them poured gallons of water from the kitchen pump on the mattress, and then, it not being an innerspring, they shoved it out the open window!

A small house next to the church, directly across from the store, was Clara Freebern's home. Traveling up to the corner intersection, where Harvey Road and Shield's Road met the main Thirteenth Lake Road, lived Clarence and Gladys Reed, and their daughter's, Barbara and Virginia. On Shield's Road, across from the Reeds, stood the Baptist Church. Mother was of the Methodist faith, but did attend services at that church occasionally. One day when Verne dropped a coin in the collection basket as it was passed along the row, I attempted to take it out. That was probably the first time I got a firm lesson about charitable work for God when I got home.

George Roblee's house was nearby the church. Other Shield's Road residents who patronized the store from time to time were: Myrtle Gardner, Byron and Lucy Persons, and at the dead-end of the road, my great-Uncle 'Dolph Shields. The land across from these houses was meadow.

People that I came to recognize that lived on Harvey Road were: members of the Gordon Harvey family, Jack Burgey, the Zufelts, and Ralph and Edith Lincoln. Frank and Annie Tyrell lived at the corner. They had two sons, Pat and Monk, and as I recall, a daughter, Viola. They were friends of my family and we saw a lot of them. The name Monk was probably a nickname. It seemed that his main reason for living was to tease me, especially by throwing my little red wagon down the embankment behind the store, into Thirteenth Brook. Then one of my brothers would have to retrieve it. One day he carried it to his home and threw it off the bridge that crossed the same brook, in front of his house. My mother felt that she must speak to his mom about these incidents. The teasing stopped and both families remained friends.

Author stands beside antique passenger vehicle of the 1920's. Photo courtesy of North Hudson Buffalo Farm, North Hudson, New York

I remember Mother, Annie, and us kids traveling to a picnic sponsored by the Methodist Church. We rode in an antique passenger-vehicle resembling the photo accompanying this writing. I have no idea where the picnic was held, perhaps beside the Hudson River, near Riparius, New York.

Martha Casterline was another patron of the store. She lived farther up Thirteenth Lake Road, on a hill reached by a long driveway. I also remember Hugh and Nettie Davis, and their boys. Their house was on Cemetery Road, near the old North River cemetery.

From my front-porch observation post at the store, I was fascinated to see Mason Davis rein in his little, brown mare in a cloud of dust. He lived near my great-Aunt Alzina Raymond's home, on School House Road. With the grace of a performing athlete, and a crutch to support his one leg, he would jump out of his single-seat buggy, ascend the steps, and cross the porch without a halt, to enter the store. Incidentally, that horse-drawn carriage may be the one prominently displayed at the world-renowned Adirondack Museum, located in Blue Mountain Lake, New York.

Another outstanding individual was Fieman, the tin-peddler. He was from out of town. His vehicle, similar to the antique one pictured, could be heard rumbling in the distance. With clatters and thuds he arrived to park in the yard.

"Here comes Fieman! Fieman's here!" my childish voice proclaimed to Dad and anyone else within earshot. Word spread throughout the community as though by Town

Author, at age four, watches for Fieman, the tin peddler, on the front stoop of the store.

9

Crier. Folks swarmed to see what he was carrying that differed from the store merchandise.

My father was partially deaf due to the use of a jackhammer on a road project when he was a young man. Because of this he often had me accompany him "to be his ears". This was true as he delivered Mother's home-baked goods to the summer people who owned camps in the area. Thus, I came to recognize some of them also: the Jays, Mullens, Stannards, and a lady, Mrs. Beardsley.

May these few names, places, and tidbits of information help connect the present to the past, for the heirs, and other inhabitants of the area.

*S*ome sounds that occurred in the evening or later in the night, left lasting memories also.

Squealing brakes, splintering wood, and a woman's scream cut through the night air. *Had a car gone through the wooden railing of the wooden bridge that crossed Thirteenth Brook in the settlement?*

"Wake up! Wake up!" Mother shouted into Dad's partially deaf ears, shaking him. "I think that someone's gone off the bridge!" He was not one to panic in the face of emergency, but the urgency in her voice prompted him to scramble into his clothes and join other men who were running up the dirt road in the direction of the noise.

I went back to sleep before he returned home, but the next morning there was much conversation about the incident among store patrons. The car had not gone off the bridge, but out of control on a slight grade leading to it, and over an embankment into the woods. If I remember correctly, a baby of the young couple involved in the accident was found unharmed on a pile of leaves.

"Lee! Lee! I need some help!" The distressed voice, coming from outside through the open window one night, was that of my great-Uncle 'Dolph. Again, Dad had to be awakened.

"Something's the matter with 'Dolph. He's yelling outside," Mother informed him.

Not fully awake, Dad groped his way to the window and shouted out, "S'matter 'Dolph?"

"Got'ta see a doctor! Can't stand the pain *no* longer. Big toe! Tried to cut it off with the axe. The pain! Got'ta go to the doctor."

With that, Dad dressed and went out to investigate. He helped Uncle 'Dolph into the car and drove away. I went back to sleep. Other than Dad telling Mother, next morning, that 'Uncle Dolph's problem was gout (a strange word to me), I heard no further discussion about it. Whether he truly had taken the axe to his toe, I never knew. At age four, *incidents out of sight or sound were out of mind* for me.

A couple of events from this time might have made the tabloids today.

"Where is he? Where is that *xbqo*? I seen him come in here!" the woman shrieked as she charged through the door of the store one evening, brandishing a hunting rifle. "I'll blow his *xplq* head off!"

Dad, kneeling in front of the potbellied woodstove to set the controls for the night, waved his hand toward the back. He gave no indication of the fact that preceding her by only moments, a young man had entered the store in the same manner.

"Lee! Hide me! Where can I hide? She's after me!" he yelled. 'Nor did Dad mention that he, himself, had motioned to the frightened man to jump over the center-counter and crawl under the recessed back side.

The woman, with the fervor of Annie Oakley, streaked through to the kitchen, out the back door, and disappeared into the night.

Awakened one night by loud voices coming from outside, I crawled out of bed and across the floor to the window. Reaching for the windowsill, I pulled myself up and peered out to see what it was all about.

There on the hillside in front of a house, was a huge, wooden cross burning. Scary flames licked upward and outward menacingly. I had no idea of the implication of the scene. Loud, threatening voices used words I was not accustomed to hearing.

Swiftly, Mother scooped me up in her arms, tucked me back in bed, and proceeded to tell me a story. I was soon fast asleep again.

The next day, bits and pieces of conversation by patrons of the store aroused my four-year-old curiosity.

"Bet he'll stay to home now."

"If her husband could know."

"It should be a lesson to her."

Although I didn't understand, it wasn't long before I pieced together that a group of self-proclaimed moralists deemed it was too soon after becoming a widow for a woman to have a gentleman caller, and it could not be tolerated.

Such is a glimpse of life in one small Adirondack Mountain settlement from a child's perspective in the early Twentieth Century.

*A*lthough Dad preferred to earn a living independently, his heart was not in inside work. He was an outside person, his specialty before the store being a sportsman's guide. He went with the hunting parties for the sake of being in the woods. He was not licensed and did not charge, but tips from grateful sportsmen compensated.

Dad, second from left, as a sportsman's guide, for a hunting party packing into Lewey Lake located in Hamilton County, New York.

Dad knew the woods for many miles in any direction. He knew the best feeding grounds of the partridge, the fall roaming of the deer—their winter yards. He knew how to get to the ponds where the beaver and muskrat lived, the tracks of every wild animal, and where their trails were likely to lead. He knew the best time of season for every species of fish, the depths of water at which they were found, and the holes in which they lay. Responsibility for the store business and the general work that went with it waited, while Dad kept the customers (many of them summer visitors) spellbound with his hunting and fishing tales.

During the throes of the Great Depression, although my parents had the store, they, too, had to pay for family groceries, meet the mortgage payments, and be accountable for store merchandise. Other businessmen also felt the pinch; this had a ripple effect. Many years later in the attic of my grandparent's home, I would find the cash register receipts of these people who never paid their bills.

13

It was a time when designer fur coats, hats, and scarves were a sign of fame, fortune and prestige in the world of the rich and famous at home, and abroad. This did not mean much to the rural people of the Adirondack Mountains, but the money associated with the trapping of wild animals for their fur, did. Dad was an expert trapper at any time of year.

My first knowledge of his dependency on this skill for extra income was when we lived at the store. He had gotten several beaver out of season. After preparation of the hides for sale, they were stashed between the surpluses of flattened, cardboard boxes we always had. When enough accumulated to make delivery worthwhile to another store about eight miles away (that served as an outlet for illegal animal pelts), Dad made the trip.

One particular day I was with him as per usual, excited that he had let me come along. We were just about to enter the place, when the local game warden was walking in at the same time.

Dad stepped resolutely around him with me at his heels and continued on to the back of the store, where he deposited the stack of boxes on the floor.

"Here's your boxes," he announced to the person in charge, and just as resolutely, he walked out with me in tow. I was privy as to what had occurred, but tagged along quietly in the order of the day—*children should be seen and not heard.*

This was not the end of the story. Contrary to what it implies, my father was not dishonest or an outlaw. Without permission, he would not have taken as much as a rusty nail from a fellowman. But conservation rules and regulations were little understood, and interpreted by many as an infringement upon a man's civil right to provide for family from the bounties of the land in ways that other work could not. This opinion was attested to by even notable persons, like the late Adirondack Hermit, Noah John Rondeau, well into the Twentieth Century. Mining companies, businesses that deal in forest products, and sports enthusiasts still question the authority of the Conservation Department today.

Dad's luck ran out when his trapping buddy was caught and turned state's evidence (plea bargained) to implicate him as an accomplice. When Dad announced to the family of this happening, the words I heard like jail and fine terrified me. That my Daddy might be taken from our home was an unbearable thought!

"No! No!" I sobbed, throwing my arms around him. If *jail* meant his leaving us, and *fine* involved money to prevent that, he was welcome to the shiny coin someone had given me. I ran to get my copper piggybank.

Paternal grandfather, Emery Raymond, in farm field.

I never knew what happened, but my daddy never left us. From this incident Mother thought it best to give up the store and return to the Dew Drop Inn. She could see the *writing on the wall:* that the economy was not going to get better soon, and might plunge them so far into debt that they would never recover.

*P*aternal grandparents had died recently and left the 39-acre farm to Dad, as an only child. Mark, his only sibling, had died of pneumonia at age 19. Dad had been commuting to care

Paternal grandmother, Rhoda (Cross) Raymond, on front steps of the farm house. Farm dog: Snyder

15

for the animals. The house was fully furnished and we could stay there while renovating the Inn. Mother hoped that in time the Inn (minus the barroom) could become a family-oriented, tourist vacation spot.

Although Dad saw the possibility of its being a sportsmen's paradise where his expertise as a woodsman and guide could reach its highest potential, he was reluctant to leave the store. For then he would have been content to keep on entertaining the customers with his wilderness stories and hope that business would improve of itself. He enjoyed being his own boss, but couldn't visualize all the work involved to start something new. Fifty-dollars a year would have to be paid to his benefactor, Harry Lincoln, until his financial obligation for leaving the store was satisfied. But there would be no overhead expense at the Inn and much of the food needed for serving meals could be self-produced at the farm, Mother pointed out, as she convinced him to make the move.

The original Inn gained acclaim when wagon teams hauling hemlock bark from the northern forest to the North Creek, New York tanneries made it a stopping point to eat and rest their horses. Stage coaches carrying lumbermen, sportsmen, and affluent vacationers back and forth did the same. Despite the Depression, business (though limited) had to go on, and the sportsmen found a way to come to the Adirondacks for hunting season. Wayside accommodations were also appreciated by the privileged few summer travelers, driving their own automobiles or using Frank Pelon's Indian Lake, New York taxi service.

A person, my folks called Art Shaunessy, had been renting or buying the Inn, but he had left. In a genealogy search years later I discovered that someone named Arthur Sans Souci had once lived there. That caused me to wonder if those two names might have referred to the same person, but I digress.

Brother, Max, had married Armenia LaPell, daughter of Dennis and Charlotte (Harvey) LaPell, and moved on for a life of his own. Verne was not too keen about leaving his classmates at the one-room school on School House Road. But I didn't care where we lived as long as it was with mamma and daddy.

I do not recall when we left the store, but it must have been in the spring as Mother wasted no time in planning the work at the Inn and assigning everyone a job. Dad quickly reminded her that he had to put in

Grandpa Emery Raymond's, little, old Model-T truck.

gardens and that Verne was old enough to be a big help.

Grandpa's little, old Model-T truck transported everything we owned in one load. Stoves, bedsteads, and large furniture pieces from the original purchase were still at the Inn. Big appliances were things of the future, as were indoor plumbing and electricity. Thus there was nothing to hook up or turn on. Surplus inventory goods from the store were left at the farm small items for cleaning were taken on to the Inn. Our lives, like this recount, would fluctuate between these two places for the next 10 years.

Author, at age three, demonstrates size of apples in the King apple tree at the farm.

My great-Uncle Frank Cross had begun building the farmhouse for his bride. When the company he worked for moved to Glens Falls, New York, he was forced to move also, or be out of a job. *Could that company have been Finch and Pruyn?* He sold the place to his sister, Rhoda (Cross) Raymond, my paternal-grandmother. A family document shows that in 1909, she borrowed $ 900.00 from J. Ordway—a successful businessman. This may have been when she bought it. I am happy to say that a receipt verified repayment. It was a well-built home for the times, having eight rooms, hardwood floors, decorative door and window casings, and a slate roof. A parlor exit-door featured a frosted-glass panel etched with the design of an elk in the forest.

An addition with no cellar (resulting in a very cold floor) was put on later, for a larger kitchen with another bedroom over it. That bedroom with four windows was bright and cheerful. Cozy warmth ensued from the kitchen stovepipe heat running through it to the chimney. But the room, although used, had never been finished.

Fresh air from open windows drove out the musty odor created by being closed up with only lath and plaster walls. Holes gouged in those walls by movement of furniture over the years would stay there, until Mother pasted muslin squares cut from flour sacks over them, and wallpapered. Until then the room would be a place for me and my doll family to play. I spent many a happy hour decorating those walls with pictures I had cut from old catalogs, and then stuck on with flour and water paste.

The farmhouse had been unoccupied for quite some time. When we arrived, there were cluster-flies in the corners of the unused bedrooms and rats lived in the dirt-floor cellar. One of the first things Mother did was to exterminate the flies by holding a lighted kerosene lamp, with the wick turned low, underneath the cluster. The vermin simply dropped down the lamp chimney to their doom.

The rats were a different story. Active only at night, their existence didn't seem so obvious until one ran across my bed as I slept, awakening me with a start! My screams woke the household, even hard-of-hearing Dad. Within seconds he was chasing that rodent around the room, making desperate attempts to flatten it with the broom. He finally succeeded when it ran under a piece of clothing that had fallen from a chair to the floor. We soon owned a cat.

*T*emporarily settled in at the farm, we began work in earnest at the Dew Drop Inn. That was a two-story frame house located on what is now State Route 28, where it still remains, approximately equidistant from North Creek to the south, and Indian Lake to the north. At 1,984-feet above sea level, the location was once determined to be the highest point in New York State over which mail traveled. Now we were back there to survive the Great Depression. Dad was looking forward to family independence; Mother was hoping to revive the business.

The house had been set on the contour of the land with no thought of leveling the ground. Thus the fieldstone foundation was over five feet high on the back. With the passage of time, some of these stones were precariously loose; some had fallen out. Mother lamented that the openings were *big enough to throw a cat out through*!

One could enter the cellar from outside through a handmade wooden door of standard height. Broken glass in the only window was partially covered by a piece of cardboard. Along the dirt floor, apple and potato bins, and big barrels of sand that once held carrots, produced lingering scents.

Visible on the opposite wall was a steep stairway, leading to the kitchen. A wide wall-shelf, at the base of the stairs, was full of empty canning jars.

On bleacher-type steps underneath the window were tall, translucent-green glass containers of liquid. Dad explained that these were batteries. When connected to the big, black motor nearby, the batteries could produce light throughout the entire house. He started the engine to show us how powerful it sounded.

"Shut that thing off!" Mother immediately shouted, covering her ears with her hands.

These two devices were never connected; the house was never wired for the magic of electricity.

Less formidable was the metal, cylindrical receptacle setting on a rickety wooden table. It was encased in a shroud of grease and grime, as was the tubing protruding from it. I wasn't curious enough to ask what it was used for.

Exiting the cellar into fresh air, the huge, flat rock I would claim for a playhouse sat directly opposite, nestled in a semicircle of brush and trees. I would nail a small wooden crate to one of the trees to hold my doll dishes. Just a step away from the rock into the woods, white Indian pipes stood erect like tin soldiers. Dainty, pink lady slippers nodded gracefully, and the beauty of the red or white trilliums was deceitful of their offensive odor. No wonder the common name for them is stinkpots.

It was refreshing to step inside the icehouse and be greeted by the sweet woodsy-smell of sawdust. The sawdust was packed over and between blocks of ice to slow it from melting in the summertime. Built into the side hill, with the earth encasing three sides like a root-cellar, the ice lasted there all summer.

Sloping land, between the icehouse and the outhouse, provided our own private landfill. Even over a decade not much refuse had piled up in it. It was not a throwaway society then. Home-canned foods were preserved in the same glass jars year after year. My family subscribed to no newspapers or magazines; any scrap paper was used to kindle the wood fires. All food unfit for human consumption was fed to the pig. When an item was worn out for its original purpose, it was recycled for some other function. Even minuscule pieces of rags were wedged into pin-sized holes in enamel milk-pans to prolong their usefulness.

Of all the outbuildings, the privy was the most important for obvious reasons. That upright structure, built over the incline, had a porch providing a level entrance. There were no windows, but a row of boards left off the top under the roof let air and light in along with spiders, beetles, and other flying insects. A two-hole bench inside was sized to accommodate both big and little folk. Dad said it needed no pit dug underneath as the excrement, neutralized by wood ashes, could roll or be pushed down the slope with other trash.

The weather-beaten siding was enhanced by wild cucumber vine and tall golden glow flowers in the summertime. If ever a scene such as this fits the old cliché, *beauty is in the eye of the beholder*, this one does. To some it presents a picture of rustic charm; to others it is a connotation of abject poverty. For those of us in whose backyard an outhouse was located, it was just a necessity.

One other ramshackle structure on the very edge of the property served as a garage, a place to hang washtubs, and garden tools. Doors askew, the weather-beaten exterior matching that of the privy, and the entire building in need of repair made it far from eye-appealing. Little did we realize how soon in this simple setting business would expand to where more accommodations were needed.

Mother had grown up with the tourist industry in the late 1800's, when the Adirondacks were discovered to be a wonderful place for rest, relaxation, and improved health. Her parents, David Erastus (affectionately called "Rat") and Martha (Rist) Farrington, operated a well-known tourist home, simply called Farringtons, on the shores of Indian Lake. Well-to-do people from the city profiting from lumbering activity and the fur trade in these same mountains, and outdoor sportsmen made up the bulk of the guests. The place is still in existence, presently called Timberlock, with a part of the original log-building in its structure.

Mother's background was motivation for her to hasten the work at the Dew Drop. All water had to be lugged by the pail-full from springs at the base of the hills on either side of the house—over 1,000 feet. This was one of Verne's jobs. He soon discovered that we had access to the well across the road where the house used to set.

It was deemed great progress when Dad built a platform under the eaves to set big barrels on in order to catch rainwater for cleaning. It was piped into the kitchen sink and once used, allowed to run through a pipe in the wall onto the ground.

It took several weeks to get the place ready for business. Soap, water, Lysol, elbow grease, and a hammer to pound in some of the loosening nails (as the boards dried away from them with age), were about all the working materials needed—all we had.

In addition to hauling water, Verne's tasks were to help with the heavy work such as: moving the furniture, keeping the woodbox filled, removing the myriad of fat, grey spiders from the porch ceiling, and cleaning the privy in a like manner as the house. I helped where possible, dusting furniture with an old rag. With Verne's help, I lettered and painted a business sign on an already painted board. I was also the gopher as I would "go 'fer this and go 'fer that" between Mother and Verne who had to share cleaning supplies.

On a bright, sunlit day with a brisk wind, we flung doors and windows open, and began work. Every vessel from the stove reservoir and teakettle, to various pots and pans, was filled with water to heat on the kitchen range. The stove firebox had to be kept full of wood.

We carried out mattresses and laid them on the green grass in the hot sunshine, utilizing fresh air and sunlight to do what Febreze, Woolite Upholstery Cleaner, and like products are recommended for today. Ticking filled with layers of: batting, feathers, horsehair, even some from grandma's day containing corn shucks, were awkward to handle, but pliable enough to get through doorways. Feather pillows were treated the same way to purify.

There were four-upstairs bedrooms, each furnished with a dresser that had a mirror large enough to reflect one or more double beds, an iron cot with fold-out legs that could be squeezed into space available if needed, and a dry-sink. A dry-sink was a small cabinet. On top sat a large, porcelain washbowl and matching pitcher. Behind the doors underneath was a chamber pot or pail, referred to as a *slop jar.* These utensils were for disposing of the used water from the pitcher or a bathroom emergency call during the night. Racks, on the sides or top, were for towels and washcloths. A nail or two, on the back of the bedroom doors, sufficed for a closet. Twelve-or-more guests could be housed at one time.

Mother swept the floors and stairs with the corn-straw broom that had been made by our totally-blind neighbor at the farm, Will Sanders. She used the tip of a dried partridge wing to get into the corners.

"When can I have the broom to lift down these spiders and douse them into a can of kerosene?" Verne yelled from the porch. The kerosene would be used later to keep the wood fires burning, and thus cremate the pests.

"In a minute . . . ," Mother answered, ". . . and don't forget the ones in the privy!" She went on to explain that when Dad bought the place it was infested with bedbugs. Using a spoon to try to eradicate them, by scooping them away from the beadings of the mattresses into a cup of kerosene, had failed. The place had to be closed up as airtight as possible and lighted exterminating candles were set in tin cans to give off poisonous fumes. I suppose family had to vacate.

Calling it dry-cleaning, Mother drew an old pillowcase over the broom and changing it frequently, wiped it across the ceilings and down the walls in very even strokes to remove the accumulation of smoke from the woodstoves and that from cooking grease. It would be years before the common kitchen fan or washable wallpaper was available. I followed her from room to room to dust the furniture.

"Shake your cloth outside like I do," she reminded me.

The only room that merited new wallpaper was the one where the roof had leaked—then, only where the leak was, as Mother knew it would ultimately be ruined again and need to be recovered once more. I had been born in this room she told me and the roof leaked down on me then. Now all these years later it was still leaking. Dad said it was too steep to be repaired. That someone must have climbed up there to build the house in the first place never came to mind. As this room was located directly above the barroom, a coat of calcimine or muresco was put on the ceiling to cover the stains there. These paints were, I believe, both dry powders which had to be mixed with water.

Before moving on to clean the four-rooms downstairs, the wooden floors (some of them uneven planks worn smooth with the passing of time) were scrubbed with a solution of water and lye soap, or a splash of lysol—perhaps both.

In spite of Mother's rush to meticulously clean the Dew Drop Inn, some time had to be devoted to survival tasks of caring for the gardens at the farm and preserving hundreds-of-jars of food for the coming winter. There were also the mundane tasks: planning and serving the daily meals, washday for the weekly laundry, and seasonal berry picking. Each proved to be time-consuming.

At every opportunity Dad was off hunting or fishing. Although only hoofed animals were considered fit to eat, we did consume a lot of squirrel, rabbit, and even woodchuck meat that summer. Before the gardens matured it was *slim pickings* for food.

"So you think we've got it tough? After the War (World War I), if a family were lucky enough to have a piece of meat, it was for the father who worked the hardest. The rest got only the broth." It was Mother's voice admonishing Verne who was staring with disdain at a pot of beef bones boiling on the woodstove.

The bones had come from a grocery store, via Howard Farrington, Mother's distant cousin. He and his wife, Hattie, collected them for the Beagle rabbit-dogs they raised. Even though a sizable amount of meat might be left on them, to sell bones was never considered. That meat, together with cornmeal-mush (served hot, or sliced and fried in bacon grease when cold) or with just plain johnnycake, made a hearty meal and the broth was an excellent *stone soup* base. The cornmeal was a portion of what was purchased in bulk from Waddells feed store in North Creek. Although it was for the pig, Mother sifted out some for family use.

"If it *don't* hurt the pig, it won't hurt us," she declared.

There was always an abundance of homegrown potatoes. Dandelion and pigweed or mustard greens helped to make up a meal. This was at the end of a long winter when the cellar shelves were empty of the canned food from the previous summer.

Stale bread-cubes and eggs, scrambled together with leftover, chopped boiled potatoes and onions, made a meal go further if unexpected company showed up. Pancakes with syrup, made only from sugar and water plus a maple flavoring if we had any, were at least adequate sustenance.

Bedtime snacks might be bread and milk in a cup, toast covered with warm milk on a plate (called milk-toast), a cup of plump oyster crackers in hot water, or thickly sliced potatoes grilled on the woodstove griddle—the latter three with a generous spoonful of homemade butter added. We never went to bed hungry.

*T*he only fruits we ever had were berries or apples. But picking berries was not my favorite pastime. The mental images of berry desserts and happenings in the fields were the only things that made it interesting.

Strawberries, being the first of the season to ripen, whet our appetites enough to put up with the black flies which were more plentiful than the berries. In no time my face would be covered with streaks of berry juice and blood from fly bites, as I tried to brush the pests away. An eye could be swollen nearly closed from a bite on the lid. Starting a fire in an old pail or kettle to create smoke was the only effective deterrent. This was called a smudge, made by smoldering the flame as a result of adding something not easily combustible such as green grass, wet pine cones, or leaves. But it was not practical to carry a smudge to the berry fields.

"Want to go berrying tomorrow?" Mother asked her neighbor, Edith, as they sat on the porch at the Inn, visiting one hot, June evening.

"OK, I hear it's a good year for them," was the reply.

Overhearing the conversation, I began to scheme up something that might make the venture more exciting.

Next morning, after the dew was dried by the sun, we took tin pans with handles and set out for the strawberry patch just a short distance from the house. We each selected a spot and bent over to pick the berries. When a few minutes had lapsed I removed a little, green clay snake I had fashioned the previous evening, from my pocket to the grass. I picked it up in front of Edith.

"E—eek!" she screamed, her breath coming in short gasps and her body beginning to sway. Mother, ever alert, took in the whole picture at a glance and helped her to a sitting position before she fainted.

"You!" Mother ordered, pointing her finger at me. "You go back to the house this minute and set on the kitchen steps where I can see you until I tell you to get up!"

I plodded along home and sat there whimpering with my thoughts. *Grownups were just no fun at all.*

Then there was the time we were looking for strawberries along the highway near our home. The mowed side of the road, warmed by the sun's rays reflected from the blacktop, was a great place for them. It was never a concern to anyone that the berries might be polluted, or had come into contact with any hazardous material, or that a person might be mugged while picking them. Verne and I filled our small containers and emptied them into Mother's larger one.

Working our way along each side of the highway, we came to a stash of tar barrels used for road repair. With typical boyish curiosity, Verne removed one of the plugs of an upright barrel to peer into the total blackness. The strong odor of hot tar permeated the air. He replaced the plug. Following behind him and being of a copycat nature, I, little sister, did the same. WHOOSH! The hot tar, forced upward by the air let into the barrel when first opened, exploded into my face and through my long blonde hair. Fortunately, it was not hot enough to burn the skin and by quickly closing my eyes, they were not damaged. The reflex of the eyelids is truly remarkable. I was rushed back to the house, where most of the tar was removed with kerosene followed by hot, soapy water. But it was weeks before all signs of it were gone from my brows, eyelids, and the roots of my hair.

Wild strawberries average about the size of the tip of one's forefinger. Therefore, it would take as long as two-hours, or more, to pick enough for a shortcake. Even with keen observation while picking, a stinkbug (aptly named) might be found among them in the pan. Hulling and washing the strawberries might take another hour, but the end result was worth the time spent.

Shortcake in our house was a full meal, usually supper. Mother baked a round, cake-pan sized, double-layered buttermilk biscuit, slathered with homemade butter between the layers. The butter was to make for easy separation of the layers, in order to cover the single bottom one with sweetened berries before replacing the top layer and adding more. The shortcake was then cut into wedge-shaped pieces and served with a dollop of our own pure whipped cream.

As the strawberry season was coming to an end, raspberries were ripening. Because they were on tall bushes they were so much easier to pick. But it had to be done more carefully, for they were comparatively soft and hollow once off the stem. The dense bushes were covered with briers that pricked fingers and clung to our clothes. An additional challenge was the yellow-jacket bees flitting among them. Following a short time of picking, Verne, who had declared in the strawberry field that he would rather pick raspberries, announced that it was blueberries, next to ripen, that he really liked to pick.

At the farm one day as Mother sat at the sewing machine, where the one raspberry patch on our property was clearly visible through a window, she glanced out and saw a big black-bear in the middle of it. She called out to Dad and me.

"So that's what's been wallowing through the hayfields," Dad grumbled. It was hard to mow the hay when it had been trampled down. He grabbed his hunting rifle and fired off a shot. He had no intention of killing the animal and only hoped to scare it away. The bear reared up on its hind legs and left. We never saw it again.

No matter how carefully the raspberries had been washed, we sometimes found an inchworm sitting on top of them after they were stored in bowls on the pantry shelf. Apparently, the worm could hide in the inside crevices of the berry to avoid being flushed out. We discarded the intruder and the berry he was on, and gave the rest another washing. Due to the scarcity of raspberry bushes in the area, we ate the few we gathered as they ripened. With a sprinkle of sugar and pure cream from the top of the milk pans, they were a snack *fit for a king*.

Open meadows or clear-cut land at the farm, promoted heavy blueberry growth. When I was 12-years-old I often accompanied Dad to the hayfields. While he was busy with the haying, I could fill a 10- or 12-quart pail with blueberries on the field periphery. Picked clean with no stems, leaves, or insects on them they could be sold for $ .25 a quart at Racket Brook Inn, on the way home. That money helped purchase my school supplies for the coming year. At our own Inn, when blueberry pie was served to guests, especially hunters, they often asked if there were an extra pie they could buy to take home. Mother usually planned to accommodate them.

It was rare to see a skunk in the daytime, but once as Mother and I approached a field of blueberries, there one sat in an upright position viewing us with as much curiosity as we viewed him. We could not tell whether it was the entrance to his burrow or if he were also berrying, so left him alone and turned away. Verne had chosen to help a neighboring farmer with haying that day and said he did not like to pick blueberries anyway.

"Blackberrying is much easier," he remarked.

Blackberries grow on tall bushes like the raspberries, but in smaller clumps. They are the largest of all wild berries and thus fill containers faster. However, the needle-sharp thorns on the berry stems can have a grip on one's clothing comparable to that of a snapping turtle. It is painful to jab one into a finger.

The best place to find blackberries was in great-Uncle Dolph's old pasture. Although it was back on Christian Hill, about five miles away, we went every season. Dad drove us there to spend the day to fill our pails. At noon, we ate our peanut butter sandwiches near a natural spring where we could get a drink of cold water. By the time he came to pick us up our pails were full.

One year after business was well established at the Inn, we were overanxious to get home. The previous night one of our setting-hens had tried to ward off a hedgehog that was after her eggs. Becoming full of quills the hen had to be destroyed, so Mother readied it for a rewarding meal after berrying.

"When do we eat?" Verne moaned, "*My belly is near touching my backbone.*"

Biscuits browned in the oven; gravy bubbled on the stove. Someone knocked on the door.

"Come in!" Mother snapped, sure that it was the prying neighbor to see how many berries we had.

The door opened and a stranger cautiously inquired, "I saw the sign. May we get food and lodging?"

"Of course," Mother answered in her polished vernacular, reserved for potential guests.

I bet that was the speediest chicken and biscuit meal, together with blackberry dumplings for dessert, those people had in their entire lifetime. As they consumed it with pleasure, we counted our blessings of the day over pancakes and applesauce in the kitchen.

"Cleanliness is next to Godliness." So read grandma's hand-embroidered plaque on the wall. Thus the Saturday change of beds and night baths, so that all would be clean for Sunday, was naturally followed by Monday as wash day.

Water was heated on a wood fire to begin wash day early. Mother had placed the copper boiler on the kitchen range. Using a long-handled, four-quart cooking pot, she filled it with water from the reservoir at the side of the stove. The already hot water from the reservoir was used to expedite matters. Before wash day was finished, over 40-gallons of additional water would be drawn hand-over-hand from the well outside and carried in pails to the house. The gravity-fed faucet over the sink, bringing drinking water in from a spring on the hillside at the farm, did not have pressure enough to fill pails rapidly.

"Fill the reservoir again," Mother said to me, as she placed the boilable whites into the copper boiler on the stove.

Having fewer clothes meant less frequent clothing changes. This resulted in heavier soil accumulating in the cloth. Everything cotton was boiled to loosen the ground-in dirt. It would take some time for me to fill the five-gallon reservoir with a two-pound lard pail lifted from the sink to the stove. I was less than six-years-old and could handle nothing heavier.

Next, Mother made the starch so it would be cool enough to immerse hands into when needed. Starching was not done via a spray can back then. It was always made from a white powder mixed with cold water to form a paste. Boiling water was poured into the paste, and the mixture was cooked, and stirred until it became clear. The readied starch was then set-aside until needed.

From adding more wood to the fire, to adding more water to each of the three tubs (now setting on wooden stands in the kitchen), wash day would be an all-day project. The fire was kept hot and steady. Other pots, pans, and the five-quart teakettle were used to heat more water for the tubs: one for scrubbing, one for a first rinse, and the third for bluing. Bluing was a commercial liquid product that helped to remove the last grime of the wash water from the laundry and enhance the fabric colors.

"Hand me the soap," was Mother's next request. With the butcher knife she shaved thin layers from the bar of handmade soap into the boiler.

I began scrubbing fine whites of linen table cloths and napkins, maybe a silk blouse or man's dress shirt, on the washboard. Up-down, up-down, turn the article over. Up-down, up-down, turn it end-for-end. Then move it on the board to the next section of it and repeat, for a washboard was only about a foot wide. One couldn't begin to count how many times the arms went up and down on the scrub board. To add more cleaning power, the bar of soap was rubbed over the item from time to time. When the water became cloudy and the article looked clean, it was swished through the suds to rid it of any clinging lint or soil, and then was wrung into the first rinse tub.

When the assorted items were ready to be lifted from the boiler into the washtub with an old broom handle, the broom having been completely worn out and sawed off, Mother took over the scrubbing as the remainder of the laundry needed more elbow-grease than what my young arms had. From the whites to the colors, men's work clothes and socks, perhaps a scatter rug last, was the order of succession—all in the same wash water. The odor from the boiler would become acrid, when grease from machinery repair, pitch from wood cutting, and barnyard scents blended together. It was tolerable only because the clean smelling lye soap was stronger.

"Why can't we have a washing machine like Aunt Gertie?" I sulked.

Aunt Gertie's washer was a round wooden tub with legs attached. The inside wall of the tub was corrugated like a washboard. One turned a handle to agitate the wash against it. *That was fun!* The wringer was fastened onto it and could be swiveled out over the rinse tubs.

"Do you think Aunt Gertie always had a machine?" Mother chastised me. "When she was your age she had to wring the things by hand. We are lucky to have a wringer." Mother tightened the wringer clamps onto the wash tub, and folded each item to the size that would fit between the rollers which removed water.

The folded item had to be as near an even thickness as possible, or the thicker part would be free of excess water and the thin area dripping. Buttons were folded to the inside and lined up flatly away from each other to avoid being broken or torn out. Everything had to be kept away from the gears at each end of the rollers to avoid grease. To operate the wringer with one hand and grasp the item going through with the other was a common knack of every housewife when doing the laundry alone. It would be years before I was allowed to feed anything through the rollers.

"But you may turn the wringer handle now," Mother said to me.

As each item was wrung from the washtub to the rinse tub, so it was wrung from that to the final bluing rinse. The wringer had to be removed from the washtub and fastened onto each rinse tub in turn. With the final wringing from the bluing water, the item was caught and placed in the clothesbasket, unless it could simply fall into it, to be carried to the lines.

At any stage of wringing, the material might become so free of excess water that it ended up sticking to itself, in the rollers. Wadding tightly together, it spread toward the greased roller gears. If grease were absorbed by the material in this process, a release lever was struck allowing one to unwind the item by hand. The grease was removed with kerosene and another thorough washing.

Articles to be starched were hand dipped in the small pan of cooled starch that had been set aside, hand wrung, and added to the clothesbasket of clean laundry to be hung.

At a convenient time we would break for lunch, usually after hanging out the whites. Clotheslines stretched on trees around the yard.

"Why should I cut more clothesline poles and cross-arms when trees are so plentiful and firmly rooted in the ground already?" asked Dad.

In the name of modesty, ladies unmentionables were hung between lines of sheets. Never would such articles of clothing be flaunted to public view! Menstrual rags (napkins or pads—nonexistent) were laid on the grass to further bleach and dry. In wintertime they were dried inside.

By the time the last tubful of wash was finished, the first ones hung out might be dry. But if the weather were inclement, all could hang for days. Brought in as needed, they were dried on clothes-bars standing near one of the stoves or mounted on the wall over the kitchen range. Clothes-bars were seldom empty, for air-dry usually meant air-damp. In winter they were often brought in frozen stiff.

The used water was carried outside in buckets, because the kitchen drain was too small to accommodate it quickly. Carrying it out was as time-consuming as carrying it in. To rinse the tubs and wringer with clean water and hang them on the side of the woodshed or garage, wipe up the kitchen floor, and keep checking to see what was dry enough to be brought in from the lines took us to suppertime. Monday was washday all day long.

When Mother was working at the farm, Verne and I often got into mischief. Principally, it was the animals there that impressed me. Verne took advantage of my naiveté.

"Run! Run!" he hollered to me when the big Rhode Island Red rooster began to chase me, and continued the chase until I streaked breathless into the house, and slammed the door behind me.

But when Verne was chased it was a different story.

"We'll fix him," he declared of the bird.

Wearing Dad's work gloves, he caught Big Red and enlisted my help to hold him while he tied a long piece of Mother's clothesline to one of its legs, and secured the other end of the clothesline to a ladder nailed on the side of the hayloft. Verne said that it would teach that bird a lesson if I ran back and forth past him just out of reach, where the rope would yank him up short when he gave chase. It sounded like a great idea to me, until Mother discovered what we were up to on the first run!

The rest of the small flock of chickens, an assortment of: White Leghorns, Plymouth Rocks, and Black Wyandots were not intimidating. For the most part they roamed freely until evening, when it was their nature to return to the hen house to roost.

We saw the big turkey gobbler grandpa had been boarding for someone go up on the front porch and leave a mess. It was one of Verne's jobs to keep the area neat and clean.

"We'll fix him!" he said. "Go get the red pepper Ma uses for cooking. I'll be right back," and he headed for the barn.

When he reappeared, he was carrying a scoop of grain. He formed a sizable mound of the red pepper and topped it with grain on the step. We moved away and waited for the turkey to discover it. The wait wasn't long. With one long-necked swoop that bird dove in to what looked like a tasty treat.

Awk, awk! Gobble! Awk! Gobble, gobble! Gobble! he sounded, sprinting with wings flapping for the watering barrel at the barn.

"What's the matter with him?" Mother was heard to mutter as she was hanging out laundry, where Verne and I were innocently playing throw and catch nearby.

When the cat's away, the mice will play. This old adage has held true through the ages. Dad was away—probably completing paperwork relating to the store business he had left in favor of tourism.

"Wanna go for a ride?" Verne asked me. He had been working all morning to free grandpa's old pony-cart from an entanglement of briars, burdocks, and brush. It had set unused beside one of the farm outbuildings for years.

"Yeah-h-h!" I responded eagerly, thinking he was going to pull me around as he used to do with my little red wagon.

He disappeared and returned shortly with Dolly, the young horse, in full harness. I had kept my distance from the livestock. Even the half-grown pig with its unfamiliar snorts and grunts was threatening. I was frightened by the looks of his corkscrew tail and his upturned snout which appeared strong enough to uproot trees. I began to have second thoughts.

Adventuresome myself however and confident that an older brother must be all-knowing, I climbed over the side of the cart and sat cross-legged on the floor. Verne backed Dolly between the fils, fastened them to the harness, and hopped aboard with reins in hand. By a cluck of the tongue and a spoken giddy-ap, Dolly pulled the cart out of its retirement into the driveway. We hardly got the cart onto the road, when a wheel fell off. There was nothing to do, but put Dolly back in the pasture and fix it. I returned to the house and my dolls.

A couple hours later I went outside. The box of the cart set separately from the lightweight wheels and axle. *Wouldn't it be fun to push the wheels around?* As I clutched the middle of the bar and ran full speed across the yard, the wheel fell off again. The one wheel remaining continued in a circle and rolled over me where I had been catapulted forward, my face in the dirt. Except for a bloody nose, a few scratches, and a lot of tears I was none the worse for wear. How was I to know the broken wheel had not been fastened on yet?

The rest of the afternoon was spent listening to Verne's tirade of reprimand to me.

"Leave stuff alone! Stay away from things! Go play somewhere else!".

So much for brotherly love by times.

Life
At the Inn

Circa 2005

*B*ack to work at the Dew Drop, meant readying the place to move in permanently. The downstairs walls, ceilings, and floors were cleaned in the same manner that it had been done upstairs, except for a coat of paint on the barroom ceiling, and one of white enamel on the door and window casings. So much paint had been put on those over the years it could have been measured for depth.

Furnishings, though adequate, were scanty—only a cooking range, table, and chairs sat in the kitchen. What sufficed for cupboards were a set of shelves on one wall covered by a curtain. A small, rectangular sink located on the back wall, had an enclosed cabinet underneath. The only plumbing in the entire house was the drain to the outside through the wall, emptying on top of the ground. A wash basin and soap dish, used by all family members, was in one end of the sink balanced by the water pail and dipper on the other end.

A swinging door led to the dining room where two sets of tables, chairs, and a sideboard were. From there, through the cloakroom at the base of the enclosed stairs, one entered the barroom featuring only the bar with shelves underneath the back side, and a potbelly woodstove near a window. The bar had no floor railing, but a line of wooden stools were across the front. Well-worn linoleum rugs covered both the dining room and barroom floors.

The largest room, on the back side of the house, served as a parlor or family bedroom if the need arose, such as when all the upstairs bedrooms were full of guests or a family member was ill. A bay window, directly above the outside cellar door, overlooked the big, flat rock I had claimed for a playhouse. My doll family and I spent many happy hours playing on the benches underneath the windows. The room was accessible through doors from the kitchen or barroom. Mother promptly placed a heavy piece of furniture behind the barroom door.

After all washable surfaces were clean, including the windows which were done using a vinegar and water solution, and then dried with crumpled newspaper, we turned to furnishing the guestrooms. Each one needed curtains, ample bed-linens, patchwork quilts, and clean equipment on the dry-sink. The pitcher was filled with room-temperature water for personal use. In hunting season this meant the water was ice-cold. A kerosene lamp and a holder for wooden matches was a must on every dresser.

Dresser drawers upstairs and kitchen shelves down had to be lined with newspapers. All items to be laundered from bedding to curtains, towels to washcloths, were washed, starched if need be, and ironed by hand. The stoves needed a coat of stove blacking, a product similar to shoe-polish. With the first fire after its application, a foul smelling puff of smoke ensued, but the result was a glossy finish.

"Remember to cover the ground under the privy seats with wood ashes and put last year's *Sears Roebuck* catalog between them on the bench," Mother reminded Verne.

I felt as though we had been at the farm for years; I was ready to move on. But Verne viewed the permanent move apprehensively. His last chore at the farm had been anything but pleasant when he saw grandpa's old cow munching his first big-boy felt-hat, like Dad's, beyond recognition. He had hung it on a fencepost nearby fearing that it might fall off his head into the thirty-foot deep well, where he was pounding in some loose nails in the curb. With the excitement of seeing it destroyed, he also dropped Dad's only claw hammer into the well. Efforts to scoop it off the bottom with the rope and bucket were fruitless, and Dad's wrath at the loss could not be forgotten.

*T*hat was the year for me to start public school and I was glad that I wouldn't have to walk out Cleveland Road, to meet the school bus as Verne had done the last few weeks of the school year in the spring. At the Inn, we would be picked up right at the door.

As I was just starting my education, Mother was ending cleaning of the Inn. So much time had been spent there, it was easy to settle in. I clung to Verne's hand as we crossed the highway to board the school bus. At last I was old enough to go to school with him. Now I would learn to read, and write letters, instead of marking thus /\/\/\/\/ between lines. I was filled with anticipation. Everything was wonderment to me. I didn't mind the 10-mile bus ride as I gazed out the window in transit. I watched each student get on the bus, and saw the house he or she came from.

The size of the school, as the driver pulled into the parking lot, was awesome. I had never been close to a big building made of bricks. Entering that building with the wide halls, high echoic ceilings, cold plastered walls, and marble floors was scary. I tightened my grip on Verne's hand so hard my knuckles were white. He marched me through those long halls to the first grade room. Prying my hand from his, he left me there.

Confidence came as the door closed behind him and I was among children my own age. That they and the teacher were strangers was not frightening to me. I was accustomed to being around people I didn't know through my parent's business at the country store.

The huge classroom filled with desks and seats, and an entire side wall of windows adjacent to one of the blackboards, was most impressive. A half-bath at the back of the room equipped with child-size furnishings was astonishing. I felt as though the noisy, gushing water when the toilet bowl was flushed could suck me down with it if I stood too close. How different from the outhouse at home! To flip a switch on the wall and have a room immediately flooded with light would have been the eighth wonder of the world, had I known about the other seven. Instant light meant instant fire in my house. I stayed away from that switch. To think that anything like these marvels could ever be in my own home was preposterous!

My major memories of first grade are learning the alphabet, and the emphasis placed on phonics when reading. Introduction to Dick and Jane and their dog, Spot, along with the *Weekly Reader* newspaper, were my main interests. I remember little about arithmetic. But it was due to a number game that I learned *honesty is the best policy*. My cousin, Ned (my same age), brought a dime to school for me to give to my mother. It was payment from his mother for a package of garden seeds. The two mothers were sisters. Walter, a classmate, had a Lotto number-game. He said I could have it in exchange for the dime. I had no games; it was an irresistible temptation. On arriving home and Mother's inquiry as to where I had gotten the game, I told her Walter had given it to me.

Later, when Ned's mother, Aunt Gertie, checked to be sure Mother had gotten the money, I was in deep trouble. Mother positioned me over her knees and gave me a spanking. A spanking was just that—a spanking, not a beating. It was never administered in anger and I got the message. It was effective until reaching the age-of-reason, which I think was sooner rather than later those days because of it.

An incident from the first time the students left the classroom is memorable. We strode down the hall in single file, turned a corner, and went on to another room, perhaps to eat our brownbag or tin-pail lunches. On the way back I knew our homeroom would be on the left so I darted through the first door on that side—totally oblivious of the fact that no one else had done so. What a shock to find myself in a boy's basement, as school restrooms were then called. I was quickly escorted out and back into the line.

During the Great Depression, parents were not always able to accompany children through traumatic experiences. We grew up with great independence, and a trust that persons in authority would look out for our best interests. Therefore, when the school dentist discovered that some of my baby teeth needed to be extracted, I was not unduly alarmed. Mother had pulled a couple by tying twine string on them and yanking. On an appointed day I was taken to the dentist's office via a school car.

I slid into the chair unaided, but when the dentist proceeded to place an ether-cone over my nose and mouth, I fought like a Bengal tiger. No one had told me what to expect beforehand. The next thing I was aware of was awakening in the chair with a mouth full of blood and Mother standing beside me. I later learned that there had been so much bleeding, a car had been sent for her. She took me to Aunt Gertie's house in the village for the rest of the day. We both returned home on the school bus.

My tonsillectomy was a like experience. According to the school physician, my tonsils needed to be removed. I was sent to the hospital by way of the welfare department. Lying on the operating table, I gazed upward at what must have been a big, round skylight in the ceiling. At that time it reminded me of a Mickey Mouse mystery story from a *Big Little Book*. Mickey had been strapped on a round cement stand in a gristmill. A disk above was to be lowered to torture him. *Could tonsils be removed like this?* My body stiffened in fright. Then the ether-cone was slipped over my nose and mouth. Unlike the results of this action at the dentist's office, I welcomed the semisweet fresh smell of the gas and was anesthetized quickly.

When I awoke with an unimaginable sore throat, I began to squirm. I was in a ward with a diversity of patients: a young mother who had miscarried (*whatever that meant*), a little girl with a chronic illness, and several others. I suppose this was the designated room for welfare patients. A nurse directed me to expectorate the accumulating blood in my mouth into the crescent-shaped dish on the bedside table. This I did, frequently. During the night Mother was brought in for me once again. I was not a hemophiliac, but apparently a bleeder. Nevertheless, I was discharged within the usual length of time for tonsillectomy patients.

These experiences were just more examples of growing up strong, attested to in a book by the same name. First printed in 1995, the book was written by four women with similar life stories, having each lived in the Adirondack Mountains.

Before my first year in public school came to an end, there was one more incident of human interest worthy of recounting. The school principal, Mr. Biha, a dark-complexioned heavyset man, came to the classroom door, requesting that I accompany him to the office where Mother was waiting for me. *My mother here in this building? No way!* I wouldn't budge. Failing to convince me, he had to bring her to the room. The occasion? Dad had been hired by a well-known carpenter to drive him to a place where he had done some outside work the previous season. It was north of the school; they would take me with them. This was so exciting—a trip beyond school !

It seemed that the carpenter, allegedly intoxicated, had lost his false-teeth in a brush pile when he took a nap. Unable to find them at the time, he had been without them for several weeks. In desperation, he decided to see if they were still there. Arriving at the destination, he was elated that the brush pile was still intact and immediately began searching. Eureka! He found them! Blowing the dust off, as one would blow out a birthday candle, he triumphantly slipped them back into his mouth—a true story with a happy ending.

Meanwhile, Mother had put the finishing touches on the Inn guest rooms, and just before deer hunting season the sign I had lettered was hung on the corner of the stoop:

DEW DROP INN
LUNCHES & ROOMS
$ .50

No sooner than it was visible, some of Dad's old cronies stopped by to see what the place had to offer and by opening day of hunting season, word-of-mouth had brought in a capacity crowd of

Lon, a guest hunter from the city, with his buck. Note the sign.

hunters. Mother abhorred the barroom, viewing its existence as *no fit place* to bring up children. But to make ends meet during the Great Depression, one sometimes had to risk being on the cutting edge of the law to survive. So it was during Prohibition which ran before, and concurrently with, the last years of the Depression. I don't know if it were permissible throughout that era to make beer, or homebrew as it was better known, for private consumption, but I know that my father and many of our neighbors did so.

Fifty-cents at the Inn provided a traveler with: a portion of meat, some home fries, something from the garden, a homemade slice of bread, coffee, and a cookie for lunch. A "complimentary" bottle of homebrew brought in a brisk business. When a pair of Revenue Agents stopped in one day, Mother caught a glimpse of shoulder holsters under half-open jackets. No questions were asked and the men seemed to enjoy the food. Nothing came of the incident, but the barroom *remained a thorn* in Mother's side.

Dad, an adventuresome young man at the time, thought that operating the "still" (that metal, cylindrical receptacle in the cellar) would be a worthy experiment so attempted to make some corn-liquor, often referred to as moonshine. He really didn't know how and the equipment was so old he ('nor anyone else) dared to drink the clear, alcoholic liquid that dripped through the curved tubing. Mother, distraught with the prospects of the venture, discovered it was good for starting the wood fires and it was used up thus.

Another of Dad's adventures, frowned on by Mother at this time, was bootlegging from Canada. A local innkeeper solicited his help in making a run, for which he would be paid. It sounded like an exciting way to make an extra dollar, so Dad enlisted the help of married brother, Max, which upset Mother even more. On the return trip, the innkeeper's car was pursued by Revenue Agents, forcing him to abandon the vehicle with its illegal load which was steered into the Ausable River at some point. He was rescued eventually by another participant. These bootleggers all had their plans for escape if possible. Dad, proceeding by another part of the plan, arrived safe and sound with his load back to the innkeeper's establishment, but the trip had proven to be more of an adventure than he had bargained for and he never tried it again.

Beer made at home was a success story. The ingredients, some of which were: malt, hops, sugar, yeast, and water were mixed in two, 10-gallon earthenware-crocks and set on chairs behind the kitchen stove to warm and ferment. When properly aged, it was poured into bottles and capped by use of a bottle-jack. This was a piece of equipment that held each filled bottle in a recessed foot plate. The bottle cap would then be tightly crimped on by lowering the handle of the bottle-jack over it. Operating the handle was my part in the "family business". I thought it was fun. It was Verne's job to store the bottles against the building, under the back porch. Concealed by wild cucumber vines which covered the base latticework, the bottles were not only hidden, but kept cool. None of the operation was kept secretive; neither was it advertised.

To Mother, serving a complimentary bottle of beer with a lunch was one thing, but to have Dad's cronies join him at the bar was quite another. Occasionally, the men would become rowdy and Mother was continually after Dad to take out the bar.

One day some outsiders of the usual crowd became antagonistic and Dad asked Verne to help remove them. Mother promptly decided Verne needed to accompany her and me to the strawberry fields, and told Dad that when we returned to the house, she expected everyone to be cleared out.

When we did get done picking berries and returned, everybody was gone—including Dad. Some furniture was overturned and a window was broken. Evidently, there had been a fight and Dad had packed those who were left with no transportation into the Maxwell and driven them to their homes.

"This is it!" Mother declared.

She took the axe to the bar and when Dad returned, the barroom was a parlor. A few of the barstools, grandma's reclining couch and library table from the back parlor, and a couple of wooden rockers from the porch were the furnishings. With Verne's help, the bar was a neat little pile of kindling in the backyard.

According to Mother, now the Dew Drop Inn would become a respectable tourist home with a respectable clientele. Dad never said a word, but he wasn't happy with the situation. He thought that a more family-oriented business would diminish his manly position as a guide and proprietor of the place.

A day at the Inn during hunting season then, and in later years, went like this: *Brr-r-r-r-rng*! Alarm clocks were ringing in every room.

"Breakfast time! Everybody up! It's on the table!" I shouted. If they had not heard the alarm, they would certainly hear me.

It was 6:00 A.M.. The help had been up since 4:00 A.M.. As the youngest of the work force it was one of my tasks to pack the lunches consisting of: two sandwiches, an apple, and a cookie for each member of the hunting party. Come noon, Dad would have the hunters near a fresh-water spring or mountain stream to *wash it down*.

Two-pots of steaming coffee sat on the back griddles of the kitchen woodstove, with more previously made and put in a quart tin-pitcher; oatmeal waited in double-boilers. Mountains of pancakes and sausages, along with plates, cups, and saucers, were in the warming oven which sat over the top of the range. Hot food met hot dishes on the table.

Eggs were fried and toast made over live coals at the last minute. To have the heat from wood coals just right, at that particular part of the breakfast hour, was a skill known only to Mother.

There was no fruit or fruit juice. That was not our custom. The only oranges we ever saw were at Christmastime, and then only one in each stocking.

Earthenware-pitchers of cream skimmed from the top of milk-pans were on the table, along with homemade butter and maple syrup.

Water boiled in a big iron-teakettle; more was stored in the reservoir at the side of the stove. The guests could carry some of it to their rooms for shaving if they cared to.

Where was the hungry horde?

I never knew such a sleepy bunch of men to come so wide-awake as their feet hit the cold linoleum floors in the unheated rooms, and each doused his face with cold water.

Bits of conversation drifted downstairs.

"If you think this is cold, wait 'til you trek to the privy!" The old-timers were full of advice for the young newcomers.

"The what?"

"What do you mean an ungodly time to get up? You gotta' get out early to get your buck!"

"Early? It's the middle of the night! Has anyone got some aspirin?" Probably meaning he had stayed in town too late the night before.

Then in two's and three's they descended to the dining room, and in 20 minutes the food it had taken two hours to prepare was gone.

The fellows donned their various hunting attire. Most wore knee-breeches of pure wool, and woolen or leather hunting jackets. Each had a rifle, a well-filled cartridge belt, and a hunting knife. Footwear ranged from moccasins to laced hunting boots. Red, back patches and hats were worn for safety.

Dad's appearance was in sharp contrast: his faded plaids as likely to be green as red, wearing his old, year-round slouch-hat, and high-cuts laced halfway, the strings wound around the boot to use up their length and tied. A piece of clothesline might be his belt, and would come in handy, for tying the feet of or dragging in the game.

As a rule he would carry no surplus bullets. One to fall the deer, one to finish it off with if necessary was enough. Dad never really believed in having a surplus of anything. Confident that he would never get lost, unable to hear signal shots answered if he did, the other shells in the gun chamber were enough for emergency: a rabid animal, a charging buck at mating time, a wounded bear perhaps.

He did carry matches (the wooden kitchen-variety) in the hole in his gun stock and a hunting knife. He also had a compass which he seldom looked at. Moss grew on the north side of a tree. When facing the sun at noon, north was at one's back, east on the left, and west on the right. Streams always flowed downhill to somewhere. Who needed a compass?

"When you leave the house, know in what direction you are going and come back the opposite. If you do ever get lost, stay in one place. When you know that you can't get out, stay put. Don't wander. Don't panic! Someone will come and find you," Dad announced in his low, but authoritative voice which could be heard among the men. He continued, "We will be in the woods by 7:00 A.M.. All guns are to be loaded outside. Keep together, single-file. Keep quiet. You and you (as he pointed out the more experienced among them, often my brothers) will help me make the drive. The rest I will place on watches. DO NOT LEAVE your watch once you are placed. Keep guns in a safe position, safety on." With a flourish of his hand to indicate "follow me", he was off.

That was the most he would say all day. He was a man of few words, and assumed everyone would listen, and would follow directions. Everyone did, if not the first time every time thereafter with one admonition, and only one from him.

The line of hunters moved out, and as the woods were directly behind the house they were soon lost to sight.

We women (mother, a sister-in-law, a hired girl, and I) breathed a sigh of relief that they were gone for the day. Our work could resume uninterrupted. My sister-in-law and the hired girl did the chamber-work. Sharing the bed-making was easier and quicker. One of them took care of the used wash water, cleaned the pitchers and refilled them, and cleaned the wash basins

The line of hunters was soon lost to sight.

and chamber pails. The other checked the oil in the lamps. A swish or two of the dust mop, and clean towels on the dry-sink racks completed the chamber work. The girls went home to attend to their family's needs.

Helping Mother in the kitchen, dusting, and sweeping downstairs were my jobs. The broom was drawn across the floors with flat, gentle strokes to keep the dirt from becoming air bound. Mother was most particular about that.

Although less than 10-years-old, I would safely dust around the hunting knives, guns, and bullets.

I set the tables and helped the hired girl with the waitress work when she returned for the supper hour. I had served my first cup of coffee at age nine—carrying the saucer in one hand, the cup filled with coffee in the other.

When I became older, I also tended the woodstoves. Our wood was never seasoned; seldom was there ever more than a day's supply. One had to keep the chunks on a deep bed-of-coals, always putting on a fresh stick when the one before it was no more than half-burned in order to get the green hardwood started. I can still hear the spit and hiss of ice on those green chunks when they hit the red-hot coals in the stove. Not a grate was left intact, 'nor a stove front undamaged by the reaction. Properly setting the drafts insured safety and a steady heat. Yes, we had more than our share of chimney-fires from the creosote-prone green wood and probably more than our share of luck at combating them.

Dad could not hear the fire crackling in time to shut down the drafts, and before anyone else became aware of what was happening, flames were leaping through the stovepipe toward the unsafe chimney. I can visualize him now as he stood atop a dresser or bedside stand to climb through the trapdoor in the ceiling to the attic. Mother would hand him a container of salt to pour into the pipe. I do not know the chemical reaction occurring as a result of the addition of the salt, but liquid creosote was forced through the stovepipe connections leaving permanent, unsightly streaks. The resulting odor never went completely away.

Mother spent most of her time in the kitchen. Bread dough, set to rise from the night before, was fashioned into several loaves, and while it raised once more, she made several pies: apple, mince, berry, pumpkin, lemon, or chocolate. The apples were from our orchard; the berries preserved; the mince last season's venison meat. The others were made from scratch, mixes being nonexistent. Many a hunter took one, or more, of

Mother's pies back to the city even though it was a seven-hour drive to the Big Apple then.

The rest of the supper (never called dinner) was comprised of homegrown vegetables, home-raised beef or pork, and wild game, if a member of the party bagged something and wished to share it. It was illegal to serve wild meat and charge money for it.

There were various pickles: mustard, saccharin, dill, green tomato, and slippery tongue. Happy day when I found out the last one had another name: ripe cucumber!

Horseradish, applesauce, or spiced crabapples (stems on) complemented any meat dish. Salads were unheard of.

Sometimes steamed brown-bread, johnnycake, or biscuits rounded out the meal. Pie was usually served as the dessert. No one ever left the table unsatisfied at the Dew Drop Inn!

One can see why most of Mother's time was spent in the kitchen.

Come 3:00 P.M., the hunters returned from the woods, usually soaking-wet from perspiration and the weather, and with ravenous appetites. It had already been a nine-hour day.

They had changed into lighter clothing and the assortment of wet, hunting togs hung around the room to dry: some on the horns of the mounted deer heads, some on the deer feet gunrack. They put their boots and socks on the woodbox. Everything was informal at the Dew Drop.

Supper was served at 5:00 P.M.. When it was over with the tired, but contented, men perched on the barstools or sprawled in various positions around the potbelly stove on the floor.

The room needed no humidifier. None of the doors or windows fit properly, and the dampness from the drying clothes made plenty of moisture.

With the *BYOB* policy of the place after the bar was gone, Dad joined the men for an after-dinner drink. Ever courteous, someone often poured one for Mother. At the first opportunity of not being caught, she emptied it into a potted plant. Her house plants thrived.

Conversation was lively . . . .

"I hoped to reduce up here in the mountains, but not all in one day!" said a hefty gentleman.

"But I aimed right at the forward shoulder," a disappointed young man remarked.

"You've GOT to stay on your watch!" the voice of seniority spoke up.

"How many miles do you think we covered?" another asked.

"Did you see the size of that track!" someone exclaimed.

"Where we going tomorrow?" was questioned.

. . . and the talk went on.

Some of the fellows went to North Creek. They gathered along the bar at the Happy Hour Saloon, next to the Happy Hour Restaurant, which was adjacent to the Happy Hour Theatre. There, Harold Butler, proprietor of the tavern, listened to the stories of the day. As with fishing tales, the big ones always got away.

Other hunting parties often joined them from: the Jim Fagan House, Bucky Burn's Racket Brook Inn, Ben Straight's Thirteenth Lake Lodge, Tony Deepe's Pines, the Dell Vanwicklen private camp, and other places farther north. Each hunting party felt their guide was the best.

All knew the territory of which each spoke: from Casey Mountain to Thirteenth Lake to OK Slip; from Hoopers Pond to Starbuck Mountain to Buck Hill, Grassy Swamp, Gardner Pond, Rock Pond, Little and Big Bad Luck Ponds—a lot of square miles and all of them to be traveled again verbally.

No wonder they were still tired next morning when the hunt began all over again!

One of the hunters, an older man with a heart condition, could not accompany the hunting party daily. Late one afternoon Dad advised him to take a leisurely walk along the low ridges of Casey Mountain, some 500-feet from the front porch of the Inn.

"Often the deer, having been chased around all day, will backtrack to a favorite spot, when they sense the hunters have left the woods," Dad told this man.

The gentleman took his advice, but did not return to the Inn for supper. Apprehensively, his friend and my dad set out to see if he might be in trouble. They found him sitting patiently with his game: an eight-point buck he had come upon in the Beech trees where Dad had directed him. Nothing was more gratifying to an Adirondack guide than a story such as this.

Many of the hunters scheduled their vacations around the November elections. As with my parents, some of them who lived in the same voting district had heated discussions about the coming election. I could see why after accompanying my parents to a local school meeting when I was only 10-years-old.

Dad maintained that those who did not get out to vote shouldn't complain about the outcome later. I was to eventually learn that Mother deeply appreciated the privilege, because as a woman she had been legally able to do so for only a few, short years. Whether it was for a school issue or a government office, they never missed an opportunity to vote if it were possible to attend.

At the meeting, an important subject matter was to be voted on. I saw that politics at any level often foster an element of *good 'ole boys* who like to have things go their own way.

One of our neighbors, an out-of-towner like us, voiced an opinion about the issue that he felt needed discussion, pursuant to the main vote. It was determined that his concern should be approved or disapproved by a show of hands. As hands were raised in his favor, it looked to me like a sea of wheat waving in the wind. It appeared that his judgment was the favorite one.

What happened? Those in control concluded that the 'ayes and 'nays were too close to call and must be settled by ballot. Slips of paper for voting were passed out, collected, and counted. The 'nays won.

One couldn't help but wonder about the outcome, had there been discussion. I was immediately encouraged to enroll as a voter when turning 21-years-old, the then legal voting age.

All work and no play makes Jack a dull boy—an old cliché that is obsolete, but nevertheless still applicable. Although recreation was simple, we had our fun times and our laughs.

"Mama! Mama! I've been struck by lightening!" I shrieked, at age six, running wildly across the yard to the house.

Of course I hadn't. It wasn't even a thundershower. But it seemed that way, when I stepped on a piece of glass and the blood gushed from my foot as I cavorted through the puddles during a rainstorm. That was the closest that children of my generation ever came to having a pool.

We spent hours catching frogs near the cool springs in the wooded area at the base of the hills, by the Inn. When we were older we could find some deep water to wade in in Racket Brook. Although there were no beaches, swimming in Thirteenth Lake was the height of pleasure.

Other times one might find us sauntering along the cow paths in the pasture shade, often breaking a small, supple branch from a wild apple tree to see how far we could propel an apple stuck on the end of it. Once introduced to this sport, vacationing city kids sometimes aimed at our livestock. Dried cow flops made great frisbees in the pasture meadows, but we had no name for them then.

We played many ballgames. Simple throw and catch could take up the better part of an afternoon.

"Annie, Annie, o-oover," one person shouted when he threw a ball over the roof of the house to the person waiting on the other side to catch it. We often played this game, although some of the mortar in the old chimneys fell out when the ball collided with them. More than once a window broke when hit.

If you never rolled downhill curled in a rubber tire, you have missed a great aerobic exercise. We had to dodge the rocks, and regain balance when the tire hit a bump or depression in the ground, and hope to emerge gracefully from it when leveling out on the flat. How we kept from breaking bones or getting killed I'll never know.

Blood trickled from the wound along my shin, caused by a coiled-spring sticking through the batting on an old car seat which we were using for a trampoline. Little flesh on one's shin allowed for easy bandaging with a strip of sheeting over a piece of salt pork. It healed well leaving only a scar.

With every passing birthday we became more adventuresome.

"What in hell are you kids doing?" Dad's voice boomed from the kitchen doorway. "You want to take Ben's chimney off?"

My cousin, Ned, and I had driven a tree-sized slingshot into the ground. The sling, made from a strip of inner-tubing, held a rock as big as our fist. It was aimed at Casey Mountain. We wondered how far we could launch it. The only problem (we seemed unaware of) was that Ben Davis' house chimney was right in our line of fire.

"Take that thing apart and put it on the woodpile!" Dad ordered. Needless to say, we gave him no argument.

Dad boarded a couple of hunting dogs for Warren T. Ratcliff, a local attorney. Family was free to use them. One evening Verne and Max (who was visiting) took the coon hound out to see what he would do. I tagged along, uninvited. Just behind the house, the dog scared up a coon which immediately scurried up a wild apple tree. Wanting to see the dog resume the chase, the boys (glad I was with them then) sent me back home to get a handsaw to saw off the tree limb. When they did so, it came down hitting the dog. He took off for home and the coon sped away in the opposite direction.

Another time after dark we heard gnawing on the back porch steps.

"That's a hedgehog," Verne told me. "You hold the flashlight and I'll shoot it."

Hedgehogs can be destructive creatures. We went out the front door and crept stealthily around the house. Verne had his 22-rifle in hand, while I lit the way. We cautiously approached the noise. I beamed the light in the direction of the sound only to see an empty, 10-gallon tin-can, with a bulged bottom, rocking back and forth in the wind producing the gnawing sound. Yes, we had our laughs.

Parcheesi, dominoes, checkers, and card games were common parlor entertainments for a family. But we seldom played any of them, for days were so busy that my tired parents went to bed early and my evenings were spent doing school homework.

I found a ouija board in Grandma's attic, but Mother would have no part of that, declaring it to be wicked. Neither were we allowed to play cards on Sunday. I never understood why, theorizing that playing cards was not the issue—that cheating might be. But why was cheating any more sinful on Sunday than any other day of the week? She attributed my attitude to what is now called teenage rebellion and the rule remained—NO CARD PLAYING ON SUNDAY! It must have been a theory related to Grandma's pronouncement that *those who sewed on Sunday would have to rip out the stitches with their nose when they got to the pearly gates!*

A neighborhood kitchen-hop provided an opportunity for people to get together within walking distance of their homes. Each couple brought a covered-dish for a meal. The hosting family cleared a room of furniture, usually the dining room. There was always a fiddler in the group and the evening was spent square-dancing.

The one I remember best was at the home of Louis and Audrey Wilson who lived in a cottage at Racket Brook Inn. It was suggested that the couples dress oppositely. For a lady to wear pants was ridiculous at the time and for a man to put on a dress was a far-out, wild idea. The ladies were pretty clumsy in their ill-fitting attire and the fellows often forgot how they were dressed when they kicked up their feet or squatted along a wall to rest out a dance. The evening was filled with laughter, camaraderie, and great food.

When we reached dating age, movies, square dances, home parties, and outdoor activities such as hiking or hot dog roasts at the old swimming hole were some past-times. No one became a couch potato.

Homemade candy during the Depression was an absolute luxury and sugar was rationed during World War II. If we did rarely make some, it was either molasses candy or fudge. The former was boiled on the stove, spread in a thin layer on a platter to cool, then cut into strips to be pulled and twisted into a taffy-like appearance. The fun began with two people stretching the strips, folding a long one in half over itself, and twisting it decoratively. It was then laid aside to cool and be cut into chunks. It had to be determined when the strips were of the right consistency for each of these stages. If fingers were buttered too much for handling, one risked dropping it; if buttered too lightly, a sticky mess brought a lot of laughter—particularly if one of the pullers developed an itch somewhere!

It was strictly forbidden during the Depression to make fudge at a neighbor's house where my brother's girlfriend lived. But on a day that her parents were to be away, she invited me to help her make some. We were just pouring it in a pan to cool, when they unexpectedly came home. She threw the cooking pot and spoon down cellar, coercing her brothers to whisk them out through the hatchway if they wanted any of the candy. She then took the pan covered with wax paper, hustled it upstairs, and hid it under her mattress.

When her parents came through the front door, smoke was spewing in the air masking the cooking smell as she added a couple sticks of wood to the firebox of the stove. The boys were quick to discover the candy and we girls got nary a morsel. Of course we couldn't complain.

*R*egardless of what Father Time or the angelic cherub of January first represented, it seemed to me that the New Year began on the day when the new school year started. The end of summer vacation, and the growing season, and the beginning of school were the most significant things in my life those days. Both of my brothers had attended one-room schools in the elementary grades. I was fortunate to begin my education at Indian Lake Central School, which had been built in 1929.

Looking forward to summer vacation on the last day of the school year, we had all chanted: *No more lessons, no more books, no more teachers' dirty looks!*

I was always eager to go back to school as it was my only opportunity to mingle with my peers, and through books a whole new world of magic and fantasy opened up for me. As other students boarded the bus along the way, I was amazed at how much taller they were than when I had last seen them in June. Now, I imagine they thought the same about me.

Everyone wanted to talk at once. Conversation centered around personal experiences of the summer. There would be no talk of travels. Many rural residents did not even have an automobile. For those who did, it was mostly used during the summer for business only, and parked for the winter until July first, when the registration would be half-price. Why! It cost $ 1.00 for just five-gallons of gasoline! It had to be conserved.

Verne did not share my enthusiasm the first day of the new school year. That I had been so excited when discovering a nest of four baby rabbits in the hayfield, and watching a garter snake open it's jaws wide one time to let offspring hide inside her mouth away from my threatening footsteps, didn't seem all that interesting to him.

Besides, he missed going barefoot and last year's shoes that had to do for one more year, if possible, pinched his feet. If shoes were absolutely needed, Mother traced a cardboard pattern around each foot and sent it with an order to *Sears Roebuck & Company*. How I loved the smell of new leather when they arrived. They were to be worn only to school or church, removed immediately upon returning home, and set to one side on the bottom step of the staircase to keep them *nice*.

Before school started it was unheard of to shop for new clothes. Mother made most of my clothes or made over hand-me-downs. But if I were lucky, I might get a new red sweater from one of the $ .05 and $ .10 stores, when my parents made their annual trip to the city of Glens Falls, to stock up on needed cooking supplies for the hunting season.

When I was in first grade (there was no kindergarten), Mother made the in-style "panty dresses" with matching bloomers. This made a too-short dress less conspicuous and provided a sense of modesty in case of a fall.

As I grew taller, last year's clothing was altered to accommodate the growth. Waist lines were taken apart, a piece of material added, and then the skirt reattached. If the addition were too obvious, a wide sash was used to conceal it. Sometimes a pretty, matching ruffle covered last year's hemline to make the skirt longer. Short sleeves were made long for warmth by using some of the same material—often muslin from flour sacks.

The only elementary school supplies needed were: pencils, a lined writing tablet, and a composition notebook. But even these were hard to come by during the Great Depression. I had never seen crayons, tracing patterns, or construction paper before going to school. What a world of revelation to use those things and bring the results of my efforts home! I lined up dozens of colorful circus and farm animals to march in the cracks of the kitchen wood floor.

The usual peanut butter sandwich made from homemade bread, a cookie, and an apple, carried in an empty peanut butter or lard-pail, was my lunch. Peanut butter and jam were considered extravagant; we had one or the other, never both. For his lunch, Verne liked baked-beans between leftover morning pancakes or bread.

Eventually (probably after Franklin D. Roosevelt became president), students were given a half-pint, glass bottle of milk during recess. In wintertime when it set outside for refrigeration before use, it would be partially frozen with the cardboard cap pushed up by the creamy ice. Having had only warm milk, right from the cow or at room-temperature from the pantry shelf, I found the ice-cold serving much more preferable.

*T*he first winter at the Dew Drop Inn, was just a premonition of those to come. The place was not half-as-well constructed as the farm. The foundation could not be banked up as it was built so high in the air. To be *banked* meant building an open box around the fieldstone foundation, one side being the foundation itself, and filling it with the insulation of the day: swamp grass, leaves, sod, or sawdust, even cow manure.

The wind whistled around and through the house, from every direction. Rags were stuffed in the gaps around the door and window casings. Sometimes overnight a scatter rug, rolled up against the bottom of an exit door, was blown back and replaced by a miniature drift of snow. It was not unusual to have the flame of a kerosene lamp extinguished by a draft as it was carried between rooms to light the way.

Woodstoves provided cozy warmth in the immediate area of the room, but three feet away the room was chilly. With no central-heat or insulation in the house and poorly fitting storm windows, if indeed there were any at all, it was impossible to have a uniform-heat throughout. All unnecessary rooms were closed off for the season. Only bedrooms with stovepipe running through them to the chimney were used.

We changed into our nightclothes by the parlor stove and then dashed across the cold dining room, where a bucket of hot coals placed on a couple of bricks in the evening gave off a minimum of heat and a maximum of foul odor, especially if Dad had found it a convenient place to empty the ashes from his pipe or spit as he was walking through. Ascending the stairs leading to the second-story bedrooms, a cold walk down the long hallway led to my own.

When we were young, Mother often wrapped a warm flatiron in a piece of flannel and put it between the sheets at the foot of our bed. We soon learned to keep our feet away from it when it got cold. I covered my aching legs with an old bathrobe that I had wound around the stovepipe to absorb some warmth. There was never a danger of the robe catching fire from such low heat.

In the morning it was back near the woodstove to dress for the day which began with a trip to the outhouse. This meant additionally bundling up in coat, hat, and boots to get there, and sitting down with the wind whistling around bare buttocks and flipping the pages of the catalog-tissue. No one had to be told to hurry. Mother had already had her turn. The hot, oatmeal breakfast she had waiting in the kitchen was the best part of the day.

I believe it was the winter of 1933 that an unofficial temperature reading registered 65 degrees below zero at the Inn. The family touring car, a Maxwell, was housed in the rickety building that served as a garage. Dad had not drained the radiator so he kept a piece of cardboard across the front of it, with an old overcoat thrown onto the hood to drape down over the cardboard to help keep the radiator from freezing. He had to drive to the farm to tend to the livestock. After placing a pail of live coals underneath the oil-pan for awhile, he still had to use a crank to get the motor started.

After that severe winter, Dad thought it best to bring the animals from the farm, to the Inn, for wintertime. This meant putting an addition on the back of the garage to house them. The purpose was defeated when numerous trips had to be made to the farm for their feed. If Cleveland Road were blocked by snowdrifts, we had to walk in from the main highway and bring their hay and grain out to the car on a hand-sleigh. At the farm there was a sunken water barrel fed by a natural spring near the barnyard, where the animals could be let out of the barn to drink. They were easily lured back inside by a rattle of grain in a pan. But at the Inn, all water for them had to be lugged in buckets from the well across the highway.

*T*he following winter, Dad declared that I was old enough to walk out the dirt road to meet the schoolbus, and it was the family who moved to the farm. This we did every year for the remainder of the business years at the Inn.

The moves were not easy. They couldn't be made until the end of the lucrative hunting season. By then there might be freezing temperatures and snow on the ground. Most cold, blustery November days when we made our annual retreat to the unoccupied farm house, a desolate scene greeted us.

The summer's burdocks and thistles covered the yard. Without year-around habitation or maintenance, the place was quickly deteriorating. Windows were broken and the porch more rotted. Woodchuck holes gaped from underneath the foundation. If a stone rolled out of the groundwork of the house with the passage of time, it lay where it had landed. The same was true of a piece of slate blown off the roof by the wind or a brick that had fallen from the chimney. Dad said it was just too cold by then for repair work.

The house had had only one coat of paint since its building, the outbuildings: a barn, hay shed, chicken coop, and the inevitable privy—none. When a board blew loose on any one of them it flapped in the wind until it fell off, allowing the wind to blow through with eerie sounds and to loosen yet another. In the course of the 10-years that the farm was our winter home, one side of the hayshed was pretty well blown away!

A grove of apple trees gave the land much added value, but were never sprayed to prevent worms or pruned. Limb after limb had broken under the weight of winter snow. The trunks had become embedded with worm holes, and many of the apples with worms: Yellow Transparent, Russet, King, Jill Flower, Dutchess—names we seldom, if ever, hear now. Here and there a frozen apple clung stubbornly to a barren branch reminding one of the once plentiful, productive orchard. For years the only lawnmower had been the wandering chickens.

The well-curb had rotted away, and the well was covered only by a piece of tin which had blown off the barn roof. That water was used only for cleaning because of a typhoid fever scare around 1915. A great-aunt, visiting from the city, contracted the disease and immediately blamed it on the water drawn from the well. If there had been any way of testing it for purity, no one knew about it then.

A real luxury in the farmhouse was the running water, gravity-fed from a hillside spring some three hundred yards away. The faucet was allowed to drip to prevent the rusted, galvanized pipe from becoming clogged. Nearly every year when we moved in, the sink drain was covered with ice and the water had run over the sink onto the floor forming a layer of ice there. Mother heated flatirons and placed them on the ice to help break it up. One of us swept the pieces out the door and the remaining water ran down through a small knothole in the floor.

Some of the incoming pipes previously repaired might have come apart, some of the drain pipes split. These Dad fixed again and again by wrapping strips of inner-tubing around them which he then fastened on with baling wire. Over a period of time some of that one-inch pipe had become two inches in diameter.

The first few winters we used only the downstairs rooms. The dining room was converted to a bedroom for my parents;

the parlor containing my grandparent's daybed was my boudoir. Verne slept in the bedroom which seemed impossible to heat on the north side of the house, so he eventually moved to one upstairs. The rest of us soon followed, using bedrooms where stovepipes ran through to the chimneys as at the Inn.

Sometimes the wind filled the paths to the outbuildings with snow and whipped it into drifts which covered the snow fences erected the previous fall along Cleveland Road, blocking passage. Road crews would have to shovel ahead of the big, Walter truck plows. As main highways were opened first, we could be marooned for a week at the farm. The temperature might be below zero for days on end, often over 30 degrees below. Wind chill was not factored into temperature readings, but the expression *cold enough to freeze the hair on a dog* said it all.

But there were good times too. When snow could be easily packed, Verne, although much older than I was, humored me to get outside to enjoy it. We spent hours outdoors building snow structures. Size was determined only by how big a snowball or a block of snow we could roll up and shape. We made snowmen, and blocks we could lift, for forts, or for a house for me and our current dog, Sandy. We also dug into the snowbanks to shape big, snow igloos. When a snowbank was high along the road, one of us would climb to the top of the back of it to play King of the Hill, not allowing the other to climb to the top. We often made a snow slide to scoot down like an otter on a mud bank. The seats of our pants had many patches.

The only outside toys we had were a hand-sleigh (I never heard it called a sled) and two pairs of skates found in grandma's attic.

"We are going out to slide downhill," I would announce—as though one could slide uphill!

The hard, frozen snow-crusts of March allowed for a long run; it took a very long time to pull the sleigh back up to the top. Because the metal runners cut into the crust of the snow, we often used flattened, cardboard boxes until the cardboard was worn to shreds. The patches on the seats of our pants became quilted as Mother repaired them over and over.

Melting snow by day and freezing temperatures at night in the springtime left small patches of ice over the marshland, near the farm. With the old ice-skates clamped onto the soles of our boots, a measure of skill was required to skate over the uneven ripples of ice which were comparable to ski moguls or to skate through the marsh stubble, but it was fun.

When a new family moved into the area with a boy about my age, his father made each of us a skipjack. It was a single-barrel stave with an upright wooden post in the center to hold a seat—a most challenging piece of apparatus. One needed a good sense of balance to start with to ride it. Lacking such took a maximum of effort to attain. However, once mastered, it was so exciting to race down the hills on that contraption.

As Dad had declared that I was old enough to walk out the dirt road to meet the schoolbus, with the 9:00 A.M. to 4:00 P.M. EST school day, catching it on the main road for the 12 mile ride to public school meant leaving the house shortly after daylight and getting back home after dark—the coldest parts of the day in wintertime.

Cleveland Road ran parallel with the main highway, Route 28. Dad owned 20-acres of land in-between, 15 of which were used for pasture. It was easier to take a shortcut through this area to meet the bus. But the frozen, snowshoe path was hard to walk on. One step to either right or left of the path on new snow meant sinking in up to my hips and an overshoe full of the stuff. Keeping my balance carrying heavy school books, a band instrument, and perhaps a portable typewriter once in high school, wasn't easy.

When the four- or five-buckle overshoes were wet inside it was a struggle to get them off, especially if one's shoe size had increased, but for purposes of economy, overshoes had to *make do* for one more winter. Clothing was more cumbersome than warm. Under-alls began with ill-fitting cotton drawers. Excess material wrapped around thin, little legs. Long, silk and wool brown stockings were pulled up over the drawers and were held up by ludicrous garter-belts. Humiliating, telltale bulges showed under the stockings. In addition to my outer clothes, a pair of grandpa's woolen socks might be slipped over my shoes before putting on the overshoes, and two-pairs of mittens were necessary. A neck scarf doubled as a facemask. A woolen toque pulled over the ears nearly covered my eyes as it did not have extra material for ear flaps.

To tuck skirts and under-slips into baggy snowsuit pants, so that one looked less like a human barrel, and keep skirts wrinkle-free was impossible. I certainly was dressed in layers. Pants were strictly masculine attire, but Verne in his often threadbare hand-me-downs could be considered poorly dressed.

Unless they were involved in winter sports, girls did not usually wear snowsuits or drawers after grade school. In high school, knee-socks were in vogue. Those of us who could not afford to keep up with fashion, rolled down our stockings below the knees and secured them with a piece of unsightly elastic or a rubber band. That meant the knees were exposed to the elements, but peer pressure superceded commonsense and I boarded the schoolbus one morning with my knees frostbitten. The better part of the day was spent in the coach's office, holding a cup of snow, replaced when melted, against the affected area. That was accepted treatment for frostbite at the time and the coach's office was the nearest thing to a school infirmary.

Bus driver's did a remarkable job of arriving nearly the same time every morning, but even minutes were crucial while waiting in winter weather. The best I could hope for was to be able to huddle near an evergreen tree out of the wind. Word among students was that if Mr. Pope, the school principal, could see the school in any type of weather it would not be closed. He lived directly across the road from it.

*D*uring one of the 1930 winters at the farm, Verne had finished the morning farm chores with time to spare before catching a ride to North Creek, where he was going to meet Max. Max lived near town, and ran shuttle weekends transporting skiers up the mountain.

Several-inches of new snow blanketed the field where last week's storm already lay. Most Saturday's meant helping with the work that was hard for Dad to do alone, such as cutting firewood or shoveling paths to outbuildings. Today would be different! Verne looked forward to it with great excitement.

"Bye Ma," he hollered.

"Just be home by chore time," Dad reminded him.

"Be careful," warned Mother.

But Verne was already off to catch a ride with a neighbor. To any adolescent boy, whose only social life consisted mainly of mingling with the other farm youth while attending school, this day would be different indeed.

Arriving at the train depot in about half an hour, his excitement heightened. Throngs of people were pouring out from the passenger cars. Brightly colored ski pants and matching plaid jackets contrasted sharply with Verne's grey breeches and long, hand-knit woolen socks. Each person carried a suitcase or two, and a long pair of skis. Big automobiles and trucks of the 1930's, or earlier, were backed up near the platform. Smoke and steam belched from the vehicles in the 10-degree weather. The people had to shout to be heard over the roar of the motors. Spotting Max, Verne waved wildly.

"Hey boy, just in time! Give me a hand with the baggage," said Max.

"Where are you taking that?" Verne asked.

"To the American Tavern," Max informed him.

"I thought you drove up the mountain." Verne's voice had a sound of disappointment.

"I do, after we drop the baggage off. Put the suitcases in the back trunk and the skis on the side." Max showed his younger brother how it was done.

Not wanting to waste a minute, five-passengers quickly packed into Max's auto. They waited impatiently while Max cranked up the motor which was reluctant to smooth out and keep running in the cold air. One stop at the American Tavern Hotel, and they were on their way up the mountain, one of a long line of laboring vehicles of different makes and sizes. Tire-chains dug into the icy incline.

Enthusiastic chatter filled the air . . .

"I'm going to try Rabbit Pond trail today!"

"This is my first trip. Are the trails steep?"

"How much farther before we get to the top?"

Verne felt the anticipation and marveled at the lifestyle these people represented so different from his own. These were city-dwellers. Local folk were farmers or miners, for whom skiing was virtually unknown. Winter recreation for Verne was a couple of hours of rabbit hunting if his daily chores were done, or bobsledding at night with the two closest, neighbor boys.

When Max shifted into second, and then into low as they neared the top of the mountain, the radiator began to boil over, but the motor was steady now. Max brought the car to a halt allowing it to idle and cool-down. The occupants tumbled out and grabbed their skis from the rack. In minutes each person had his skis strapped on and was gliding down the mountain out of sight. Verne watched in utter fascination.

"Let's go! We've got to be at the bottom when they get there," Max announced.

On the steep and icy grade, the descent was almost as slow as coming up.

From the base of the trails looking upward, the thrill was even greater. The skiers approached at what seemed like breakneck speed. Crouched forward into the wind, they sailed across the flats to the parking space, coming to an abrupt halt in a swirl of snow right in front of Verne.

"I've just got to try that!" he vowed.

As Max drove him home at the end of the day, he was obsessed with the thought of owning a pair of skis. For him it was not a simple matter of walking into a sport shop and purchasing a pair. There were no sport shops in the country, and for a farm boy of the 1930's it was unthinkable to spend money for sporting equipment.

"You should see *them* skiers come down the trails!" said Verne, monopolizing the conversation as they sat around the supper table.

"Sounds like a waste of time to me," Dad answered nonchalantly.

Any activity that did not produce something of a material nature was a waste of time to Dad—an opinion shared by most rural farmers of the Great Depression era.

"Wonder they don't all kill themselves," was Mother's opinion on listening to his vivid description of speed.

But Verne was not to be daunted. He would have a pair of skis and soon.

Next morning the path to the barn became a ski trail to him. In his imagination, he watched skiers soaring over the rolling snow-covered meadows. His special work today was to bring firewood from the woodlot to the house on the sleigh Dad had made. But his mind was on skiing and he pondered how to get a pair of skis.

Verne draws a load of firewood to the house on the handmade sleigh.

They're just boards with turned up ends like sleigh runners. He knew that Dad made sleigh runners from a white ash tree. *I'll make a pair!*

After loading the limbs on the sleigh, he would usually climb on top and ride the downhill grades. But this morning that seemed too slow to be fun. He would hurry to finish his task and then look for a white ash tree. He dragged the load of firewood to the house, and on the return trip brought along a saw to cut down the tree.

It didn't take long to find the perfect one: straight, strong, tall, and about six-inches in diameter. Looking at the fallen tree, he reasoned that a seven foot length would suit his purpose. He measured off the length.

But a seven-foot hardwood log is heavy and impossible to balance alone. *Would Dad help saw it into boards on the table-saw used for cutting hardwood chunks?*

"Dad, I need some help," Verne said, approaching his father.

"Yeah, what're ya' doin'?" Dad questioned.

75

"I'm gonna make a pair of skis!" Verne replied.

"Yeah, how ya' propose to do that?" Dad replied, with some disbelief.

Verne explained his whole idea.

"Well, every growin' boy has a certain amount of tomfoolery ideas. What da' ya' want me ta' do?" Dad asked him.

With skillful handling, they soon had the log turned into two, slim boards with the scrap useful for firewood.

"Now to shave the ends to look like a ski," Verne said, drawing a picture of what he thought they should look like.

"That can be done with the adze," Dad remarked knowingly.

"I'll soak them in water to soften the wood so that I can turn them up, like you do with snowshoes," Verne interrupted.

As Dad deftly handled the adze, Verne realized he would have to do very little sanding. He gained a new respect for the man who at times seemed so aloof and tyrannical.

The next step was to fill the copper boiler used for washing clothes with water, and to fill the woodstove with wood to maintain a steady heat underneath it.

"You can't do that now. The family is coming for Sunday dinner and I need to use the entire stovetop for cooking," Mother stated.

Though Verne did not realize it, this was a lesson in patience from Mother.

"Can I soak them overnight?" he asked.

"You'll have to tend the fire," she responded.

That would be no problem. After the big meal of the day, he began the process. Into the boiler of water went the front ends of his half-made skis. They were top-heavy, so had to be fastened upright.

"Put that wire in the metal circle that holds the stovepipe up there," Mother ordered. "You know, I have just put new wallpaper on the ceiling."

The water boiled and the steam rolled; the skis would be supple by morning. They could then be bent over a rafter in the woodshed and weighted into position until dry. Everything set, Verne went to bed to dream of the skis that would soon be finished.

Rising twice overnight to check the water level and the fire, he returned to bed, and dreamed of swooping over the hills of the snow-covered hay fields on his new skis. Sure that he would be the first to awaken next morning, he did not set his alarm as usual. But his vigilance with the fire and the anticipation of owning his own pair of skis had overtired him. When he did fall asleep, it was to be soundly.

A scream from the kitchen brought him wide-awake. His feet hit the floor and he was downstairs in an instant to an unforeseen incident.

"Just look at my new wallpaper!" Mother wailed.

"What happened?" Verne's spirit momentarily sagged like the wallpaper which hung in semicircle-strips resembling upside-down knolls with two, straight boards sticking upright through them.

"The skier is in trouble already!" Dad exclaimed with dry humor.

Mother could see absolutely nothing funny in the situation brought about by the steaming process.

But Verne would have his skis. The wood had softened enough to bend for perfect tips. They would be strong and give him a proud sense of accomplishment. He had to work many long-hours for a neighboring farmer to earn enough money to buy new wallpaper for the ceiling, but it was worth it. Such was the price one boy of the 1930's had to pay for his skis.

My first (and only) pair of skis was a gift from one of the houseguests that frequented the Dew Drop Inn. Long-skis were the norm then. That pair was also seven feet long, and fitted with conventional leather bootstraps. At my height then (of 4 foot, 10 inches), today's skier can imagine the challenge it was for me to master the art of skiing. My feet slipped from side to side, and without benefit of poles the snow-angels of childhood became indentations of youth. There was room for no more patches on the seat of my pants. It wasn't long however before I could skim over the snow with Boots, our farm dog, devotedly trying to keep up.

*M*ax and Verne trapped in wintertime when there was less work to be done on the farm. Although cross-country skiing was not yet popular, they sometimes used skies to check their trap-lines for water animals around Gardner, Grassy, and Prear Ponds. Treading through deep snow on long, wooden-framed snowshoes was an arduous task. A pack-basket laden with necessary equipment such as an axe, ice chisel, and extra traps was heavy and cumbersome when bushwhacking. Gliding along on skis was much easier.

The extra traps came in handy if a new colony of animals were discovered. Then too, it was not unheard of for a beaver to get the trap free of its setting and swim away with it. In that case the trap had to be replaced.

Max borrowed my pinewood skis. They were considerably lighter in weight than Verne's hardwood ones.

"Gonna take a lunch?" Verne asked of Max on one such trip.

"Naw', we'll stop at a hot *dawg'* stand," Max quipped, ridiculing the question.

Like the experiences encountered when hunting or fishing, their ventures left everlasting stories with my family. It seemed that Max, as the firstborn sibling, often got into trouble trying to make his way in Dad's footsteps. One of his first trapping adventures, when young, resulted in a happening that haunted him for the rest of his life. He learned of homemade fox bait which among other ingredients contained strychnine. He mixed up the concoction and set a baited trap in the meadow where he had observed foxes digging through the snow for mice. What did he catch? Dad's beloved rabbit-dog, Bessie! I don't think Dad ever forgave him.

A youthful Maxwell scrutinizes the landscape.

Dad's beloved rabbit dog: Bessie

In Verne's case it was the time when he and his friend, John, teamed up to check their beaver lines. They decided that it was more practical for them to go their separate ways and meet up later on the trail. Verne headed out for the beaver dam on Gardner Pond and John proceeded on to Prear Pond outlet. When their paths joined, John was carrying two-medium-sized beaver from Prear, and Verne had found a big one in a trap at Gardner. They congratulated one another.

"That's a beauty, buddy," said John.

Then the men retraced their steps out of the woods back home, John carrying his two beaver and Verne lugging the big one.

Folks at the house were as eager to see the catches as the young men were to show them off.

"What do you think of these?" John asked, holding up his prizes. Then he remarked, "Look at the one Verne got!"

"It's yours too John," Verne said. "I *seen* you had your hands full and couldn't carry it."

My brothers, both considerably older than I, were grown with families of their own by the time I reached my later teens. Occasionally they visited back home and were amazed to see that I had an animal pelt, or two, stretched over the drying-boards they had left behind. They marveled that I, a girl, had acquired any skill in trapping. They never knew that any skill I possessed to capture wild animals was only the ability to pick up undamaged road-kill.

We always moved from the farm, back to the Inn, as soon as weather in the spring permitted. By Decoration Day, as Memorial Day was then known, the last remnants of winter ice had flushed out of Prear Pond, behind the Inn. My parents always looked forward to a good catch of speckled trout there soon thereafter.

Dad had an old, unpainted boat which he left at the pond, together with an anchor fashioned from a piece of clothesline tied securely around a rock. Little else was needed: the oars, a cut wooden pole or steel rod, a can of worms (meaning, as a rule, the flat can that Prince Albert or Velvet pipe tobacco came in which was about the size of the back pocket of a pair of pants), and a pail useful for bailing out the boat or carrying fish home in. Pulling and pushing that heavy, old scow from its mooring into deeper water surely tested our muscle power.

With the advent of spring the fish were active and hungry. One could quickly get the limit allowed, in size and number. They provided sumptuous fare after having depleted our winter meat supply. Family ate the smaller ones and near suppertime displayed a line of the big ones in view of passing traffic. No, it was not for enticing a traveler in for dinner. The fish did not hang long enough to spoil when some business acquaintance, seemingly with more money than scruples, would stop by. The string of trout looked tempting to a passerby, who having spent the day fishing farther north at one of the better known lakes had had no luck. Dad knew this.

"What'll ya' take for 'em Lee?" the person would ask.

"Can't sell 'em. 'Gainst the law," Dad answered.

But when he turned his back, the fish disappeared, and as much as $ 5.00 was left on the dining room table or bar. Dad went to town and bought some needed staples, five-gallons of gas for the car, maybe some scratch feed for the hens, and returned home with change rattling in his pocket.

Verne and I fished for bullheads at night by the light of the moon and a barn lantern. Bullheads, known as scavengers, were bottom-feeders best caught in schools near marsh beds.

We didn't always use fishhooks, but made lures by threading night crawlers onto twine string which we then rolled into a ball about two inches in diameter. They were called bobs, unlike the modern, floating plastic ones that are used today for a different purpose. Holding the bob over the side of the boat, deep into the water, several fish might latch onto it at once. They could be pulled up and simply shook off into a pail.

Another way of attracting them was to empty a bag of sod or some kernel corn overboard. As worms crawled out of the sod or corn floated in the water, the fish also bit onto the baited hooks. This may have been illegal, but there was no size limit or number of bullheads that could be taken at one time and we usually got a pail full. By the time they were cleaned, the edible part was only four or five inches long so many were needed for a family meal.

Anyone who has ever caught bullheads knows about the sharp barbs on each side and the one on the back of the fish's head. Some fishermen use pliers to handle this kind of fish; some take several minutes to grasp one to avoid getting pierced with one of those needle-sharp barbs. Anyone in my family could reach into a full pail of bullheads without looking and quickly lift out a single fish, seldom getting stabbed. Laid flat on a cutting board, it took just two-cuts with a sharp knife while grasping the head behind the side barbs to completely strip the fish of head, skin, and entrails leaving it ready for the frying pan.

Regarding brook fishing—that was something else! Bite! Swat! Splatter! Itch! Scratch! Oops! My hook was caught on an overhanging tree limb. I was trying to coordinate casting the fishline with the onslaught of black flies. It was difficult to keep the cast low where it would land on the water far ahead of one's self so as not to alarm the fish in either direction. Of course, the deep pools shaded by an overhanging tree root or a rock were where they lay, and were an easy spot to get entangled. I spent as much time freeing the hook from the surrounding bushes as I did fishing. That scared the fish and ruined any opportunity of a catch that did exist in many spots. However, it was a tremendous way to build patience, and provided a true Adirondack experience.

A small brook crossed our property at the farm. I could always depend on catching one, sizeable brook trout per day from the only deep hole therein. Improbable as it sounds, my tiger cat always accompanied me and sat on a flat rock in the middle of the brook while I fished there. That brook emptied through a culvert under the main road, into Racket Brook, from which one could nearly always get a

Tiger sits on a flat rock in the brook.

nice catch. I had gotten my limit of 10 there one day and was walking home on the highway. Of all people, Jack Farrell (the local game warden), stopped to give me a lift. I had recognized his car in the distance before it was abreast of me. Not being sure if my fish were all legal in length, I slipped the shortest ones down my fishing boots. They were clammy, cold, wet, and wriggly—but QUIET!

Every fishing trip with Dad was a learning experience in one way or another. One day hiking into Bad Luck Ponds, over a once-used logging road, a fine mist filled the air. We continued on, hoping that it had not affected the fishing. By the time we got there the air was clear, but for whatever reason the fish were not biting. I decided that was why the ponds had such names.

A picnic table on shore had shelves underneath containing some ingredients and cookware for a fish fry. One jar contained what appeared to be white cornmeal. I had heard of such, but never seen any. Curious as to whether it tasted like yellow cornmeal, I wet my finger, stuck it in the jar, and then in my mouth. It was soap powder which I had never seen either.

When traveling on a narrow, woodland trail (some of it crossing private land) to Black Mountain Pond, Dad always

stopped to say hello to the summer resident owners, the Gewhers. It was probably a mile to the pond. Fish were biting well and we had almost caught our limit when a thunder shower ended the luck.

Display of speckled trout from Black Mountain Pond.

The rain stopped as abruptly as it had begun, but the fish did not bite again. On the way home, Dad, a chronic nature lover, called my attention to the beautiful, woodland flowers, the ginseng root gathered for its medicinal value, and the protected trailing arbutus.

If a noise, unheard by him, brought something into my view, I would touch his arm and point. That day it was a mother partridge and her brood of chicks. They were almost the color of the groundcover, under and through of which they vanished. The mother bird characteristically fluttered ahead of us, feigning a broken wing to lead us away from her flock.

A fish story wouldn't be complete without a tale of the big one that got away. I was pretty well grown into adulthood and working at Thirteenth Lake Lodge, when it happened. A couple of family friends showed up on my afternoon break to ask if I wanted to go trolling for lake trout in Thirteenth Lake, bordering the resort property. I jumped at the chance!

One person set up a pole for me and then proceeded to operate the motor attached to the boat. Suddenly, jerk! went my line, going out several more feet before I had presence of mind to set the hook and begin reeling in. I kept the line taut, and waited for the driver's buddy to net my trophy. He had not wet the net first, and it ballooned upward as he immersed it in the water. In a hurry, I tried to lift the fish into the boat—a fatal mistake. With one twitch of its head it was off the hook and on the way to freedom, the big one that did get away.

*N*o matter where we were living—at the Inn, or the farm, a daily chore was checking the kerosene lamps. Safety was always a major factor in the operation of these lamps. Stored on a special shelf, high on the kitchen wall over the sink, each was taken down at night according to choice and need. We never used a lamp during the day. Work requiring light was done near a window.

I treasured a small lamp with a pear-shaped, cut-glass base which held about a cup of oil. Mother told me it had been grandpa's. By setting it on an overturned, empty coffee-can (shorter, but larger in circumference than the ones are now), it produced a larger area of illumination to do schoolwork by.

The lamp for the kitchen table had a pedestal. The smooth, clear-glass base, hexagonal in shape, held a pint of oil. It also had a larger burner and wider wick which determined the size of the flame, and gave off a soft warm glow near the old-fashioned easy-chair, a standard piece of furniture in nearly every country kitchen.

The lamp most often used in the parlor was made of pure white milk-glass, decoratively designed. It also boasted a pedestal about eight inches tall. Each upstairs bedroom had its assigned lamp and fancy kitchen-match holder.

Kerosene lamps had to be kept clean and in proper working order. Periodically, glass chimneys had to be washed and the lamp bases filled with oil. Every couple of days, wicks needed trimming. This could be done using scissors, but just pinching the carbon away with thumb and forefinger was less wasteful, and the rounded corners when done this way glowed more softly than squarely cut edges. Either a wick turned too high, or improperly trimmed, or a malfunctioning burner allowing the wick to move up automatically would cause a lamp chimney to blacken.

When a wick became too short to reach the oil in the base, its life could be extended by sewing a scrap of cloth, permitting capillary action, to the bottom. If oil were in short supply, water was added to the base of the lamp. The oil rose to the top allowing a few more hours of illumination. Thus, the last bit of wick and the last flicker of light from the consumed oil prevented, absolutely, any waste.

One lamp was treasured so much that it was kept in a closet on a high shelf out of harm's way, and was brought out only on holidays. That was a Rochester lamp which had a large spherical, ornately-designed, hand-painted glass base and matching shade. Inside the base was a solid brass, mini-tank for oil. This lamp was a wedding present to my parents in 1908.

Rummaging through the attic one day I found a tall, chrome-plated, metal lamp with a round wick that had to be trimmed with a special cutting tool. Inquiring about its origin and use, I was told it was called an Aladdin lamp. It required a unique mantle to attach to the burner in order to operate. I asked Dad if a mantle could be purchased, and why we didn't use the lamp.

"Yeah, you can *git* one from the hardware, but it's not for us. Costs too much," Dad replied and dropped the subject.

Out of curiosity, one of the first things I ever bought when I was 15-years-old and had my first summer job was a mantle for that lamp. It was $ .35 which was expensive considering my earnings of just $ 1.00. The illumination from the Aladdin lamp was far superior to that of the conventional, smaller lamps, but Dad let me know that when I became an adult and had my own home I wouldn't *live so high on the hog!*

Some people had oil lamps that sat in wall brackets. Reflectors on the back of the brackets diffused the light of the lamp. We owned none of these, but when family developed a tourist trade we did have a Coleman gas light which hung on the wall, as much for reasons of safety as for wide illumination. As the name implies, these lamps used gas and needed double mantles and a minute generator which worked mechanically by pumping air into the base with the gas. When functioning properly they were an excellent source of light, but the exposed mantles pulverized at the slightest touch. A good deal of the time that small generator was plugged making the flame flicker, producing uneven light—and it was noisy.

I mustn't forget the barn lantern. It was made of metal with a heavy glass, barrel-shaped chimney (always blackened), but protected somewhat by top and bottom brackets, and a framework that held a carrying handle. Many a fire was started by careless use of these lanterns around the barn.

*M*other remembered peddlers who walked through carrying their small wares in pack-baskets on their backs. But by the late 1930's transportation was more modern and goods more diversified. Herb Galusha carried meat in his ice-cooled pickup truck. The Chester Meat Market provided the same service. One day as the latter left our yard, the improperly-latched rear door of his delivery truck swung open. Shortly thereafter our dog, Sandy, retriever that he was, came bounding onto the porch with a brown paper-wrapped, 10 pound slab of bacon between his teeth. He had chewed the corner of the wrapping and not finding it to his liking, had brought it home to add to the pile of his other collectables. Reasoning that no one else would want the partially opened prize, my family kept and used it, viewing it as an *act of God* that we were meant to have.

A linoleum peddler brought patterned rugs and collected worn, woolen garments to be sent to the Olan Woolen Mills, where they were made into beautiful carpets for the parlor. He had a reputation for trying to charm the ladies and being too persistent with Mother one day, after being warned that Sandy would be set on him if he didn't leave, he did go minus the seat of his pants!

One traveling salesman traded stationary and envelopes for old rags. Calling at our home, he inquired of Mother as to whether she had any.

"Yes, but I'm wearing them!" she answered with matter-of-fact rural humor, an indication of the early post-Depression days.

Spices, extracts, salves, and patent medicines were distributed by a salesman for the Rawleigh Company. In our house, spices were kept on one end of a kitchen shelf, and medications on the opposite end. One day Verne made a cake, and by mistake used Rawleigh's liniment for flavoring. The aroma as it baked was most unappetizing and the loss was a financial blow to the family. The result brought a change in location for medicinal supplies.

The Fuller Brush man arrived regularly with his assortment of: veggie brushes, scrub brushes, bottle brushes, and the like. For some reason, he was the brunt of many traveling salesman jokes.

Since my parent's livelihood at the time depended on the tourist trade, Mother appreciated the opportunity to buy extra farm produce from Jimmy Jacob's traveling farm to home, open-bed truck. His vegetables, fresh from the garden that morning, were among the biggest, cleanest, and freest from insect damage that I had ever seen. The National Biscuit Company bread man would also stop at private businesses. I believe that bread was $ .10 a loaf. When summer tourists were renting our log cabin and asked us to buy an extra loaf of bread for them, I charged them $ .11 thereby making a $ .01 profit. Mother would have scolded me for that had she known.

Jake Seagle bought rather than sold, but sometimes he bartered. He had a half-ton truck with a red, open rack, and purchased junk and animal pelts. We collected old iron to sell to him and my brothers trapped small game for the same purpose.

About once a year Indians from a northern reservation came through to sell rustic plant stands. Mother traded a shotgun that had been Grandpa Farrington's for a couple of the plant stands. She did not want Verne to have it because it *kicked like a mule* when it was fired.

I would have had more siblings had they all lived. Babies were born at home; that an older woman arrived at the same time was deemed a coincidence. When Mother rested thereafter, for a few hours, it was just because the new baby needed special care that was tiring.

If older siblings were told at all that a new baby would soon arrive, it was to be delivered via the stork or brought in the doctor's bag. At the precise time of the blessed event, Dad usually placed as much distance away from the scene as possible. He always had an emergency to attend to with the animals, even if it were 2:00 A.M.. If it were daytime we young children were hustled outside, or into a far corner of the house to be entertained by an adult or older sibling.

Most of a new baby's wardrobe had been made by Mother. It began with a double-breasted cotton shirt with wide ties. The ties fit through slots in each side of the shirt and were pinned flat in the back. The bellyband was a strip of muslin about four inches wide and long enough to fit firmly around the baby's abdomen. Mother doubled the material with all seams turned inside. It covered the navel while it was healing, and was thought to keep it from protruding with growth or rupturing if the baby coughed too hard. It too, was pinned for size.

Diapers were made from the good part of a worn, outing-flannel blanket or soft absorbent material. Big safety pins, fastened through the shirt, pulled over the belly band, and pinned through the diaper itself, held all in place.

A pinning blanket was a long garment with a yard or so of warm material gathered onto a waistband, and was pinned to fit around the waist. The extra length was folded up over the baby's legs to the waist for added warmth.

Long petticoats, pinned at the waistline, fit over all of the above. Long dresses or gowns, for either boys or girls in infancy, were outer garments, sometimes with tiny buttons at the neckline or pinned to size. Yes, one needed lots of safety pins! Baby blankets were folded diagonally so that a flap covered the baby's head, wrapping the fully clothed newborn snugly. Most of the time when a diaper was wet, so were all the other garments. Rubber pants were not an option and plastic ones had not yet been invented. Disposable diapers were beyond anyone's imagination.

A bassinet was a piece of furniture of the future and poor folks had no cradles. The newborn was placed on the bed or the couch, surrounded by pillows for a barrier, or put in a wicker clothesbasket on a pillow. Sudden Infant Death Syndrome (SIDS) was not yet a household word. The little one slept in the parent's bed at night for warmth.

Mother was very adept at carrying her infant in one arm while doing housework with the other.

In so far as possible, babies were always breast fed. We siblings accepted that as a fact with no questions asked. However, the first time my own preschooler (who had seen only bottle fed babies) observed a neighbor's baby being breast fed, she later asked, "Mommy, when it is empty, how does it get filled back up?"

If a breast pump were needed and there was none to be had, the mother used a jar that had been filled with boiling water. Once emptied, a vacuum was created for the purpose.

Sitting in front of the open, oven door of the kitchen range, Mother bathed the baby on her lap. There were always cold drafts in the big, old house. An infant would certainly have suffered a chill if immersed in a tub or the sink. Each garment was removed separately, the infant bathed and powdered, and a clean garment put on before moving to the next part of the body. Before replacing the belly band, boric-acid powder was sprinkled on the navel to help it dry and heal.

No matter how many washes and rinses the diapers were put through, babies had frequent diaper rash. Corn-starch helped to sooth and heal the affected area. At the other end of the spectrum, cradle-cap on the infant's skull was a common problem. In later years this was thought to be caused because the infant's scalp had not been washed at all, or because soap used had not been rinsed off adequately. Butter, used as a cream, softened this dry skin and it was then easily washed off with a warm, damp cloth.

By the time the child was cutting teeth, he/she might be handed an empty corncob, the bare bone of a chicken leg, or even a pork rind to chew on. Of course, Mother was always present to keep a watchful eye on this practice.

"*Green Christmas—fat graveyard,*" was Grandma Raymond's dire prediction of yesteryear and it did have some merit. Lack of snow providing insulation around drafty, old homes was probably one cause of more colds, pneumonia, and influenza to which the very young and the elderly succumbed with no such thing as antibiotics.

Children's discomforts, from aching legs at night to a stiff neck on arising, were called growing pains. General aches and pains in adults were all lumped into one category—rheumatism. However, treatment for these maladies was often successful.

Some early medications left in the store inventory included Celery King and Ginger Tea, both powders to be mixed with hot water and proclaimed to be good for everything from easing the misery of a cold to menstrual cramps. Pain Queen and Sloan's Liniment were both rub-ons for rheumatism. Pine Tar was an effective cough syrup. A thick white lotion used on horse spavins was declared to be effective on human joints by some folks. Lydia Pinkham, referred to as a *Baby in Every Bottle*, was a vegetable compound formulated to make a woman feel young.

For infants, Save The Baby was a chest rub for relief of a hard cold that might develop into pneumonia. Ipecac was used to induce vomiting when necessary. Castile or Ivory soap for the bath could also be used (in the form of a small sliver) as a suppository for babies to relieve constipation.

Mother Gray's worm medicine was a tried and true remedy for pinworms. In pill or powder form, it was dissolved in water to be drunk with much distaste. Lack of proper sanitation made it easy, especially for children, to be infected. Mother said it was a sure sign of infestation when a child's lips were encircled by a white ring. In addition to giving us a dose of Mother Gray's, she rubbed a touch of turpentine under our nose to breathe theorizing it prevented the worms from working their way up into our throat.

To promote general well-being I was subjected to a teaspoonful of cod liver oil after breakfast, every morning. YUK! Often I wore a camphor sack to school as a necklace to ward off the common cold. I hated the medicinal perfume it generated—even more when it was replaced by a flannel cloth on the chest, saturated with turpentine and lard. That did make breathing easier, but in later years was proven to subject the lungs to deeper infection by keeping the pores open.

Hot mustard plasters or onion poultices were applied to the chest when congestion became severe and body temperature rose to the point of delirium. These were made by heating moistened ground mustard and putting it in a pocket laid over a piece of flannel. Fried onions were used in a like manner. They were very effective in helping to clear the lungs.

Besides a spoonful of chicken fat, one of honey and lemon usually eased a cough, but did nothing for the one I had every year from October to May. It was worse when lying down. Many nights I sat upright against the high, iron-headboard of my bed in order to sleep. Some years of grade school I missed more days than I attended, because of that hacking cough. When in attendance I was seated in the back of the room, because the teacher couldn't be heard above it.

From my parent's bedroom to mine, Dad could not hear, and since there were no symptoms of serious illness, Mother didn't worry. No one ever surmised that I was allergic to wood smoke until I was grown and discovered it for myself.

Cigar smoke blown into an aching ear was comforting. Puffball dust squeezed up the nostrils helped to stop a nosebleed. A teaspoonful of salradus dissolved in a glass of water relieved indigestion. Salradus was the common bicarbonate-of-soda. Witch Hazel was applied to insect bites.

When Verne stepped on a rusty nail Mother laid a piece of salt pork over the wound to draw out the infection, as she had done for the gash on my leg. A slice of beef steak over a black eye appeared to reduce the swelling and lighten the discoloration. A finger that had been shut in a car door was immersed in an Epson Salt solution. The nail usually came off, to be replaced by a new one.

Iodine, a brown liquid antiseptic, was always on our medicine shelf. The sting of its application to a scrape, abrasion, or puncture wound made one forget the initial hurt. Mercurochrome was a kinder and gentler version that served the same purpose. A black Icthamol ointment drew out the core of a boil or a deeply imbedded sliver.

Verne and I had all the childhood diseases. We were usually confined to bed, but a doctor was never needed. We were both ill at the same time with red measles, sharing that all-purpose downstairs room at the Inn. Seeing Verne, I remarked that I was glad my face didn't look like his. Mother handed me a mirror. Our temperatures must have been high for we were so thirsty she remarked that she was going to put a pail of water with a siphon in it beside our beds. The days were so long with the shades drawn to shut out the bright light.

I was stricken with mumps one year, when the Inn was full of hunters. They all left, except an elderly gentleman who said he had had the mumps as a child. The following year he told us he had been very ill after returning home. Dad also caught them from me and tied a woolen sock dampened with kerosene around his neck to keep them from *going down*—his own idea of treatment.

Every summer I suffered the so-called seasonal complaint of dysentery and vomiting.

"She's been eat'n too many green apples," the elders declared. After a first bite I hated green apples and I had never bitten into one again.

Home remedies, such as a few drops of oil of wintergreen with a bit of sugar in hot water or burnt toast tea, were ineffective. Even a dose of castor oil (because the body needed a good cleaning out) didn't help. For that illness I always needed to be seen by Dr. Carrol who had brought me into the world in the first place. He prescribed some big, brown fuzzy-looking tablets, each to be dissolved in eight-ounces of water and drunk at intervals. The solution looked like swamp water and was vehemently bitter to my young taste buds. Mother called it perry gork. I think the medical name was paregoric.

After any illness, Mother always sprinkled a pinch of powdered sulphur on a hot stove griddle, believing the fumes produced purified the air in the house. Although technology has provided more effective and pleasant tasting medications today, we can't help but remember that the old-time remedies produced no harmful side effects.

The flu made its rounds in a year of the late 1930's. I was sick for a weekend, but managed to attend school the following Monday. When I returned home that night, Mother met the bus with a milk-pail in her hand.

"You will have to ride down to the farm on the bus, tend the stock, milk the cow, and walk back," she informed me. "Your father has come down with the flu, has set up the old army cot behind the kitchen stove, and took to his bed."

I'll never forget that venture. It was downhill nearly all the way to the farm which meant the walk back would be mostly uphill. Since the school day ended at 4:00 P.M. those days, I would be walking home after dark. Satan, the cow, sensed that I was afraid of her. Kneeling behind the stanchion, reaching through to hold the pail with one hand and trying to milk with the other, was not very productive. Ultimately, she kicked the pail out of my hand and I arrived home with only enough milk for next morning's oatmeal.

Mother also succumbed to the flu. Max came to take care of the animals, hitched up the horse and sleigh, and drew up a load of four-foot wood from the farm to the Inn for the woodstoves. Due to the epidemic, school closed and I spent my vacation cutting that wood into stove length pieces with the bucksaw.

*F*ranklin D. Roosevelt became president in 1932. His administration was instrumental in bringing the country out of the Great Depression with the programs of his New Deal, three of which soon benefited my family.

As for Depression city soup-kitchens or breadlines (which they were most often called), we experienced none of these. But since our main livelihood was from tourism, we were indirectly affected by poor business. There was never enough money to buy new clothes or food that could not be grown.

However, with home-grown potatoes and meat, even if the meat were that of wild animals, we thought that the family ate well. That is until I doubled over with agonizing pain one spring morning while following Dad around the farm fields. He thought I might have stepped on a bee's nest.

"I've got a pain in my belly," I said in anguish as Dad picked me up and carried me, screaming and writhing in agony, to the house.

We had no phone, so Mother told Verne to run to Gid Sanders, our only farm neighbor, and call Dr. Carroll in Indian Lake. He didn't have to be told twice, but he returned to say the doctor wasn't in and couldn't be located—probably on a house call where there was also no phone. I was still screaming.

"There's a woman doctor in North Creek," Verne hesitantly volunteered the information.

"A woman doctor?" Dad shouted in utter disbelief. "That won't do *no* good!"

"Well, you gon'na let her die?" Verne asked defiantly, disregarding offspring respect completely.

"It's better than no doctor at all," Mother reasoned. "What's her name?" she asked of Verne, as if it mattered.

"Dr. McNeely," he answered.

"Well, go call her. Quick!" Mother said, concerned that I was showing no improvement.

Dad stomped out heading for the barn, a customary action if he could not control the situation. I remained in agony.

Dr. McNeely arrived in about half an hour.

"This child is undernourished," she announced, after conducting as thorough an examination as possible.

"What do you mean undernourished? She gets her meat and potatoes every day!" Mother, deeply offended, stated.

"But she needs fresh fruits and vegetables," the Doctor explained.

"The garden will soon be ready, and the apples and berries ripe," Mother quickly told Dr. McNeely.

Neither the seven basic food groups 'nor the Food Pyramid was common knowledge. The doctor left some medicine and departed.

"I told you a woman doctor wouldn't do *no* good," mumbled Dad, having returned from the barn and been told what the doctor had said.

The medicine eased my pain, but the next day a caseworker from the Welfare Department showed up. She gave us an order to pick up a list of groceries from Guy St. Marie's store, in Indian Lake.

"I can't afford this stuff!" Dad roared.

"You don't have to pay for it," the lady quickly informed him. This comment only added *insult to injury* in the eyes of my independent parents. Dad abruptly informed her she could leave.

"This child will not get better without this food," she emphasized. Sensing his fierce pride, she asked, "Would you go to work away from home if you had a job?"

"Of course I would," he answered, not wanting anyone to think he wouldn't do something to help his only daughter.

She gave him an appointment with the office managing the Works Progress Administration (WPA). With other local men, he was employed in building the road from Indian Lake to Speculator (New York). We did get a couple of food orders through the Welfare Office, but were soon able to purchase what was needed with the income Dad made from the WPA job.

Sometime thereafter, Verne joined the Civilian Conservation Corps (CCC), where he was sure to get three-square-meals a day and be usefully employed.

"Get 'em *growed* up enough to help around the place, and they leave home," Dad growled.

Dad disliked being beholden to anyone. He was used to setting his own hours, doing a job his own way. With hunting season fast approaching he quit the WPA job, and decided to build a log cabin to increase the tourism business. Logs were drawn from the farm woodlot, to the cabin-site below the Inn, by our workhorse. I do not recall which horse it was. We had several over the years: from, appropriately named, Dynamite (that we did not keep for long) to our last horse, Dan, a true gentle giant in spite of his 1,800- to 2,000-pound frame.

Like my Dad, I loved being outdoors so helped with much of the construction work of the cabin such as peeling bark off the logs, and holding one end against another as he lifted each one into place. Once the structure was up, the logs were chinked in-between with moss. Only one of the many species of moss gathered in pack-baskets from the Adirondack woods was suitable for this. For steps, thick slabs of fieldstone were drawn into place by the horse.

An outhouse nestled in the woods out back completed the construction project. A box of wood ashes with a shovel, for covering the waste, was placed in a corner. It was BYOTP (bring your own toilet paper!) if the guests wanted the luxury of bathroom tissue.

The big, main room of the cabin was furnished the same as the bedrooms in the Inn. The screened-in porch was fitted with a table and chairs, some shelves that sufficed for cupboards, and a three-burner oil stove for cooking. It was rented almost every night during the summer and weeks on end in hunting season. As of this writing, the cabin still stands and continues to be used by hunting parties during hunting season in the Adirondacks.

*S*ome sharp memories remain in one's brain as on a computer disk. Two, summertime events leaving such memories took place near the Inn, while we lived there. Either could be from headlines today, proof that history does repeat itself.

CHILD KIDNAPPED: I was playing outside one day, when a little girl tumbled out of the big, black shiny car that stopped to let her go. Screaming between stifling sobs and trembling with fear, she flung herself into my arms. I wasn't much bigger myself, although older. The two, elderly people in the car simply drove away with no explanation.

I recognized her as a child from school and knew where the schoolbus stopped at her home each day. Mother, with always an eye out for what I was doing, appeared on the scene to see what was happening. I told mamma that two, "old folks" had let the child out of a big, black car. I knew her name was Virginia and where she lived. Traumatized from it all, Virginia was unable to tell us more.

From my information, Mother recognized her family and their location. Since we had no phone she went to neighbor Edith's house to call Virginia's mother, and tell her where her little girl was, and that Dad would bring her home when he came in from work at the farm. By that conversation, it was learned that Virginia had been with her mother picking berries near the highway. Evidently, she had wandered within sight of the road, and been picked up by strangers.

We never knew if it were an abduction considered unwise later, or if the people thought they were doing a kind deed for a lost little girl by bringing her to civilization. There was a house and a service-station before getting to our place. It does seem that if there were no ulterior motive, they would have stopped there or taken a moment to explain to us. Were they fearful of becoming involved—a worrisome possibility that has always been a concern of mankind?

At any rate the story had a happy ending as Virginia recognized her house when we pulled into the driveway. There are no words to adequately describe the joy when a mother and child are reunited, or the satisfaction of being a part of bringing it about.

ATTEMPTED MURDER: I went to the door to let the cat out and lock up for the night. In the twilight, my eyes caught the figure of an apparent hitchhiker on the highway. It happened that Dad was out, and Mother and I were alone. It was unusual for anyone in the area to be stirring about at this hour of the night. We only had one neighbor, so I quietly locked the door and extinguished the kerosene lamp. We went upstairs to our bedrooms.

As previously stated, the Inn was located on a hill over which traffic had to pass. We could hear a car ascending the hill from the south. Within moments men's voices were heard to shout, although the words were indistinguishable. The shouting grew louder indicating an argument. A man's bloodcurdling scream pierced the air. Thundering footsteps crossed the porch. We could hear furniture being overturned and splintered. Someone banged on the door and Sandy barked furiously. I shook so violently I could hardly crawl through the hallway to join Mother. We both stood paralyzed with fear as we hung onto the tall iron-headboard of the bed.

Pulp trucks driven at all hours of the day and night made up much of the traffic going by. We could hear one laboriously chugging up the hill from the north. All voices and activity from outside quieted down. The truck groaned over the top. Gears were shifted down to a slower speed as it began to descend the other side. Then with more shifting down and loud squeals of the brakes, it ground to a stop. All was quiet until it started up again.

Just then Dad came home. I ran down the stairs to meet him. Choking back tears, I incoherently tried to explain what happened, pointing to the pushed out screen of the dining room window where Sandy had probably jumped to chase the intruders.

"Daddy! Daddy! Get your gun!" I pleaded.

"We'll see what went on in the morning," Dad simply remarked, as nothing was happening then and he, not being party to the occurrence or one to get excited easily, did not feel the need to investigate.

I climbed into bed with him and Mother for the rest of the night. I was about 11-years-old.

At daybreak a gentleman drove up and alighted from his car, together with a younger man. Both came to the door, the older man inquiring as to whether anyone had heard a ruckus outside the previous evening.

"No, no. We didn't hear anything," Mother hastily answered—that fear of getting involved surfacing. Dad stepped closer to hear what the man wanted.

"Tell him. Tell him what you heard," he encouraged Mother.

She related the events of the night before, and the gentleman, in turn, informed us that one of his twin sons had recently met up with bad company, and gotten himself into the situation of being stabbed in the shoulder. With that, the younger man pushed back his shirt to reveal a sizeable bandage.

Upon surveying the scene where this allegedly happened, we saw evidence of blood stains near the mailbox, and on our porch, where the victim had evidently tried to escape his attacker by entering the house. Failing to do so, signs of a flower box, of potted geraniums and ivy, knocked off its brackets indicated he must have jumped over the railing to get away from the dog.

The pulp truck arriving on the scene had apparently scared the assailant away. The driver either recognized the bloodstained person who had staggered back onto the highway, or was just a Good Samaritan who had stopped and given him a ride to the doctor's office in town.

Not to be forgotten (although I have no details) was the robbery of Jim Fagan's filling station and road stand on Route 28, just three miles north of the Inn. It was rumored to have been committed by the same persons who attacked the young man near our place.

Less dramatic, but nevertheless significant, was when two, old cars chugged northbound up the hill, one summer afternoon. By the way they were dressed, we recognized the occupants to be a band of gypsies. From open windows in the vehicles peered so many children that I likened the scene to the nursery rhyme, *The Old Lady That Lived In a Shoe*. Later we could hear the children and see puffs of smoke over the hill where the barn, belonging to the original Dew Drop Inn, had been. We realized that they must be setting up camp for the night.

With preconceived notions from stories of gypsies being thieves, who stole everything from clothes off clotheslines to little children, I hoped that they would stay over there. I never heard my parents make any derogatory remarks about them, but Mother agreed with Edith that she was glad to not have a washing hanging out.

Next day, after we were sure they had left, Verne and I walked over to see where they had camped. The area was neat and clean with evidence of only some tall, wild grasses having been cut (probably to use for making baskets), and a small, circle of stones that had contained a campfire.

*P*roducts of the environment in which they lived, my parents were staunch characters. Dad looked to the serenity of the mountains to ease life's burdens, to live as free and independently of society as possible, and carry on. Mother, forced to *make-do* to survive: used her ingenuity to become self-sufficient, faced each day bravely, and was eternally optimistic.

"Knowledge of death is so very much a part of life," she stated matter-of-factly. Maybe because at the premature birth of one of her girls, she was told by the country doctor that she would never have a daughter who lived.

Of the several born to her at home, and the last one in the sterile atmosphere of a hospital, I was the only one to survive. Dad was heard to remark more than once that it was the contrary disposition that came with me. But of several sons, only two brothers lived also. Thus, I attribute the doctor's diagnosis to more than gender.

My own first encounter with death is only the memory of Dad going for Edith, and of her being with us for a few hours. Mother had fallen, and the baby I had been told would be coming soon to live with us had been stillborn.

I sneaked into an upstairs, closed-off bedroom to gaze in awe at the lifeless little form: fully developed, fully clothed, and looking to me like a doll. I crept stealthily out and closed the door. A little inner voice said to me *don't touch*, alerting me to the great miracle of birth and death, letting me know that this was not a doll.

I made absolutely no connection between Mother's temporary illness and the stillborn child, some different from a preschooler today. Nevertheless, from the experience came a sense of maturity and growth that no educator or TV program could better. When the little corpse was laid to rest in a secluded part of our own land, beneath a blooming apple tree, the lesson that life contains some sorrow was instilled forever.

"Dan went down to the pond at noon to fish and he isn't back yet. I wonder if something could have happened to him," Edith informed Dad, providing my next memory association of death.

Dan was Edith's husband. If fish were biting, it was not uncommon for local folks to stay long hours at the pond, but it was nearing suppertime.

"I'll go see," Dad volunteered.

Dad returned to the house in 20 minutes. He had found Dan sitting in an upright position against a giant Beech tree: *stone dead.*

When I saw my friend and neighbor, he was lying neatly dressed in a box called a coffin. Although I did not understand, the silent tears of relatives and friends revealed to me that this was a sad occasion and something very final. No one explained; I asked no questions. Life went on, and as the sadness of death was overcome by the vitality of life, must be death truly was a part of life to be accepted.

That each ordeal strengthened us for the next one was surely true in my young life, when I was faced with the greatest loss of all to date: the death of my only living sister. It happened while I was at school. The doctor's son told me, when he returned from lunch at home.

"You're lying," I vehemently disagreed, and shook my head in disbelief.

When Dad met the schoolbus that night, I knew the truth.

"I know. I already know. Shirley Marie's dead. She's dead, ain't she?" I blurted out, convulsing in tears. The look of amazement on his face as to how I knew was quickly followed by one of relief that he did not have to be the one to tell me.

I quietly entered the room, where her body laid waiting for a casket. A penny covered each eyelid to hold them closed. Edith sat with Mother.

I wanted no supper. My heart was heavy as a rock. I followed Dad, where he retreated to a nearby hill to sit on the ledges and stare aimlessly at the distant pond. Ants scurried in and out of the cracks in the stone, carrying their dead prey. A field mouse scampered under the leaves to evade the hawk circling overhead. Some life went on; some didn't. Why did it have to be this way? Why? Why? In childish anger, I crushed some of the lively ants underfoot.

When the sun set behind the hill, we turned and walked in unison toward the house. Not a word had been uttered. To have spoken would have meant to have shouted in Dad's deaf ears. I hesitated to break the silence. Words were not necessary anyhow. This was a time of reverence. In the natural order of things, the sun would rise again tomorrow. With the pastor's help, death could be taken care of. Life must go on.

*O*ver a period of time we came in contact with many different personalities whom we never might have met otherwise. During the first, full summer of business at the Dew Drop Inn, the strangers who stopped by were often hitchhiking transients in search of work. On seeing an Inn, that might be a good prospect for getting a handout, they often asked. Most were humble in their request. Regardless of how they inquired, Mother never refused.

Among them was a young man who over a year later sent two, $ 1.00 bills with a note of gratitude for the lunch Mother had given him. He must have found work and been extremely grateful, for $ 2.00 was a great deal of money back then.

The homesick boy, still in his teens, whom Dad found curled up in the back seat of our car one morning, had run away from the CCC camp in Blue Mountain Lake. He did not ask for anything, but Mother could see that he was famished. Dad told him he could split some firewood for his breakfast. He was from New York City, and his attempt to do so was disastrous. Dad convinced him that if he didn't even know how to split wood he probably would never be able to get a job, and advised him to ride back towards camp on the schoolbus when it stopped for me. Of course to Dad, having been born in these mountains in the 1800's, knowing how to split wood was every bit as important for a man as learning the three Rs.

It was very rare to see a black man in the vicinity, but during this time one appeared at the door. Mother was down back in the garden, and I was alone to answer his knock. I might have panicked, but for an incident when I was four-years-old.

We were on our way to town three- and one-half miles away. This was a special occasion, and I was allowed to wear my first store-bought dress, sent to me by my great-Aunt Olive, who lived in Glens Falls. Dad slowed the car to give a lady walking a ride. When she turned to get into the back seat with me, I observed that she was black. I bolted over the back of the front seat between Mother and Dad, causing him to struggle to keep the vehicle on the pavement.

"What in hell are you doing?" he exclaimed. He knew she was the maid for a wealthy, summer resident.

"I don't want that black to get all over my new dress!" I sobbed.

Getting back to the man who had knocked at the door of the Inn. He asked only for a drink of water to which I willingly obliged.

"Why didn't you holler to me?" Mother asked, when I told her what had happened. "He probably was hungry too."

Mother went on to tell me about her first-awareness of black people. It was at Farrington's, her parent's, tourist home. A young, black man accompanied his wealthy employer as his valet. He was welcome to stay, but had to room in the cellar due to prejudice by the other guests.

As the economy improved under President Roosevelt's New Deal programs, working people traveled to the mountains to communicate with nature—putting it in modern terms. These tourists brought the outside world to our door.

One lady, of German heritage, gazed at the face of Casey Mountain and remarked that where she had lived in Germany, a mountain like that had been terraced to grow crops. We stared at her in disbelief. We thought of the herds of deer we saw grazing in the clearings of that mountain daily, the bear that occasionally ambled across the top, and the bald eagle that circled high above it. The eagle would dive straight down and as swiftly up again, with prey in its claws to carry to its young nesting on the Blue Ledges of the Hudson River. She returned several times to spend a few days with us, and her brother came every hunting season.

Another woman told us about the Seeing Eye canine school she was involved with. Memory recalls that she was from New Jersey. The following year she wrote for a reservation and addressed the letter to: Mr./Mrs. Coleman—Dew Drop Inn. Our family name was Raymond. She must have been impressed by our Coleman gas lamps.

A tall, lean Texan stopped for an overnight saying that he was on the way home after spending several months at the Trudeau Tuberculosis Sanatorium, at Saranac Lake, New York. He returned there periodically for a checkup, and always spent a night or two at our Dew Drop Inn.

All the places these people were from sounded so very far away to us.

Regular guests, year after year, were the hunters who reserved as much as a year in advance. Most of them were policemen from New York City. We always called them cops. The word *policeman* was foreign to our vocabulary. George was one of the most exceptional. He had a radio in his car. That was such a marvel to Verne and me that we always spoke of George's *radio car*. Sometimes he took us to the movie in town, always turning on the radio for our enjoyment. I remember so well the antics of the Three Stooges, and the talented Shirley Temple on the Happy Hour Screen. In the summertime George brought his family to stay an extended length of time in the cabin.

Then there was Pete, the practical joker. One time he arose in the middle of the night to take an old, deer foot and make a set of tracks across the front yard of another hunter's camp.

Henry was another unforgettable character, not for anything remarkable about his personality, but because he discharged his hunting rifle in the house when unloading it.

The bullet went through the ceiling, where another guest had just stepped away from his dresser. To unload a gun in the house was absolutely a crime, and Henry was ordered to pack up and leave immediately.

An Italian gentleman came regularly every fall and returned again with his family, for a month come summertime. Dad partitioned off some rooms in the house to provide an apartment for them. They often invited me to dine with their children. The meals were delicious and much of the fare was like ours, albeit sometimes prepared differently. One day when I spotted a cleaned chicken head bubbling in the pot with the rest of the chicken, I was a bit taken aback, although my mother always cooked the feet. They also picked black cherries from the nearby trees and showed us how to make wine.

In retrospect, with all the people who came our way also came an introduction to a diversity of cultures and lifestyles, greatly broadening our view of life beyond the Adirondacks.

Home
On the Farm

*T*ourism had been our livelihood, often at a sacrifice. But I believe the income was secondary to the pleasure my parents felt in providing a service. It was nearing another hunting season and we were busy with the regular tasks of harvest when a neatly-attired gentleman appeared to shatter our peaceful existence.

"I am a representative of the State Department in Albany," he introduced himself, holding out a page of credentials. "In the interest of public health and safety, rooming houses from now on must have safe lighting and indoor plumbing," he went on.

"What in hell are you talking about?" Dad questioned in not too gentle a voice.

Mother quietly pondered the situation, in the background as housewives did in those days.

The gentleman reiterated his statement, handed Dad the explanatory set of rules and regulations, and took his leave. Dad promptly sat down to study it to see if he had heard it right.

"Never! Never! will the State tell me how to run my business!" he declared with an oath.

"I don't see anything healthy about putting the privy in the house!" Mother emphatically remarked after reading the information provided.

Both realized that this hunting season would be their last at the Dew Drop Inn. There was no alternative, but to move to the farm.

Other hardship factors entered the decision to leave the Inn. With America entering World War II, many things were being rationed: sugar, meat, other foods, gasoline, and tires among them. There was a freeze on automobile production. All this affected tourism.

I didn't look forward to a permanent move to the farm at all. Staying there winters and walking out Cleveland Road, or through the shortcut path to meet the schoolbus had been a tolerable situation, when I knew we would return to the Inn, and tourism. Life would be so dull without the vacationers.

Besides, I was beginning to fantasize about dating and was sure that no boy would find me at the farm. Little did I know then that the favorite haunts of young men were back roads. I was so antagonistic about the move that my parents finalized the business of the Inn during my spring recess, when I was visiting my great-Uncle Bernard Beakbane's home, in Glens Falls.

Mother had repaired and papered the walls of the unfinished bedroom over the kitchen which was for her and Dad. She also newly papered the one over the parlor that was mine. I persuaded Dad to put up a wide shelf on the long wall, and position a pipe between the brackets holding it up. I made a cretonne curtain for the shelf to form a closet. Cretonne was a brightly colored fabric, usually imprinted with a huge flower and vine design. Talk about flower power!

Mini corner-shelves were the perfect place for school books and papers. In addition to a double bed with its high, fancy-design steel headboard, there was an antique desk carpentered with square nails. It was tall, with a hinged drop-leaf covering small, divided shelves which were useful for storing school supplies. The drop-leaf, when lowered, made a comfortable writing surface. Grandma's swivel, organ stool served as a desk chair. Four windows provided sufficient light, even if it were cloudy outside.

The first thing I did, after reluctantly accepting the fact that we were at the farm to stay, was to make a sign to be erected at the corner where Cleveland Road met the main highway. It indicated that North River village could be reached either way. I hoped fervently that some traffic, if for no reason other than curiosity, would reroute by the farm. It didn't. School became even more important to me. I never wanted to miss a day.

Thoughts of my future loomed up in front of me. My parents had only an eighth grade education, all that was required of their generation. Max and Verne had both quit school at the legal age of 16. I had an incredible urge to graduate from high school and go on. But to what? The only honorable choice for a girl was to be a teacher, nurse, or secretary.

To me, in Junior High, the war was something happening to someone else in lands far away. But I realized there must be a great need for nurses, and decided that's what I would be. Scholastically, that required a college preparatory course. In addition to the mandatory three- or four-years of English, I must take three-years each of mathematics, science, French, and history, along with some electives.

My parents didn't seem overly concerned about the loss of revenue from the tourists. Dad was cutting pulp that he had a ready market for, and he was planning to put in bigger gardens from which to sell farm produce. He had already been asked about apples. A few bushels could still be salvaged from the sad-looking trees.

*I*t was a relief not to be obliged to commute between residences. We no longer had grandpa's old cow, Molly, only Satan—whose name portrayed her temperament.

"C'boss! C'boss! C'boss!" I sing-songed, when Dad sent me to round her up and drive her into the milking yard. Within two-feet of it, she might bolt and head back for the open meadow. Sometimes I covered most of the pasture three times before completing my mission.

Once Satan was in the yard, Dad grabbed the milk stool, sat down with his head firmly against the hollow of her hip, and proceeded with the milking. She shook her head and flicked her tail, sometimes into the milk pail (one could only hope it had no manure on it), and impatiently stomped her feet. Under his breath Dad uttered an oath. When he finished, I lowered the bars of the milking yard and Satan left posthaste.

Dad strained some of the milk through a clean white cloth or cheesecloth, into quart milk cans. I delivered those on foot to two summer cottages in the area. The milk went directly from the cow to the customer with no thought of pasteurization, and was another small source of income.

Dad was not abusive to the farm animals; neither were they pampered. Their care was strictly a matter of business. In his opinion the cow was a beast of burden, and to milk her was an act of kindness so she wouldn't be uncomfortable and suffer mastitis. The only niceties she ever got was a salt-cake placed somewhere in the pasture, or maybe to be sprayed with a fly repellant before leaving the yard.

Satan was the most obstinate critter we ever had. She was a fence jumper and once when she was about to freshen, Dad fitted her with a poke. She jumped anyway and within a few hours her beautiful bull calf was born. It was healthy and stubborn as its mother. Eventually, Dad sold them both to Herb Galusha, the meat peddler.

Satan twitches her tail in protest of poke necklace.

Another bit of revenue was made by renting pasture rights to F. B. Burns, owner of Racket Brook Inn, for his cow. I knew him by the affectionate name of Uncle Bucky, although he was not a blood relative. What a difference between his big, brown cow, Moo Moo, and Satan! There was also sharp contrast between the owners of each cow.

HONK! HONK! HONK! Three blasts of Uncle Bucky's car horn was the signal to Moo Moo that a pan of fresh vegetables and apple peelings awaited her in the milking yard. In a few minutes she ambled out of the woods, along the edge of the brook, and across the meadow to willingly enter the yard. She gave a plaintive moo as if to announce her arrival. Uncle Bucky sat down on the milk stool by her side. With a wet cloth he carefully wiped off her udders before beginning to milk. She contentedly chewed her regurgitated grass cud, and he chewed his tobacco.

When he finished milking he coated her udders with vaseline, and with a hand sprayer applied anti-fly spray to her body. I often hung around to raise and lower the yard bars for which I always received a coin. As if to say adieu, his cow mooed again and moseyed out toward the woods. One readily understood why she was called Moo Moo. Uncle Bucky poured the milk into cans for use at his own Inn.

Each cow produced 10- to 12-quarts of milk, twice a day.

*T*he farm kitchen was approximately 13 feet by 15 feet in size. I can't imagine walking the distance from stove, to table, to cupboards today. Neither can I imagine the size family this was planned to accommodate (my great-grandparents had 15 children). Mother must have walked miles just doing ordinary kitchen tasks. No wonder there was an easy-chair near the stove, where she could grab a moments respite while food was cooking or a baby nursed.

Of a practical nature though was the location of the rectangular, cast-iron white-enameled sink, with the high splash-back. Located on the back wall adjacent to the stove, water could be passed from it to the stove reservoir while standing in one's own tracks. To muffle the sound of the continuously running water, the dipper handle was positioned in the water pail so that water trickled down it. One could always get an ice-cold drink.

"Why get new pipe?" Dad asked as he continued to wrap strips of inner-tubing around the leaky pipes. What was good enough for grandma was good enough for us.

On the drain-board left of the sink to the wall were two bars of soap: Mother's homemade lye soap for laundry; and Proctor and Gamble (P&G) for dishes. In later years a red box of Duz soap powder was a new and improved product for laundry. *Duz Does Everything* was its slogan. Additional items on the drain board might be: Old Dutch Cleanser (a powder for scrubbing stubborn burns on pans or spots elsewhere), a bottle of Lysol, a wire dish scrubber, and a couple of brushes: one for bottles; one for cleaning vegetables.

On grandma's washstand between the sink and back door was the family, enamel washbasin, alongside of which was a holder for Ivory soap. A couple of nails in the side of the door casing held a towel and a washcloth used by all family members. Below these on another nail hung Dad's respected leather razor strop (pronounced *str · ŏ · p*, as grandpa had called his, not strap). His porcelain shaving mug, with the shaving brush and straight-razor in it was kept on the high lamp shelf. A family comb sat in a holder underneath the wooden framed, oval mirror above the washstand.

On the wall across the room opposite the stove, a wide-countertop separated floor to ceiling cupboards. A swing-out, 100-pound flour barrel, and baking pots and pans were kept in the lower cupboards. The serving dishes on the top cupboard shelves were accessible to either kitchen or dining room, through doors that could be opened from either side. These cupboards covered the entire wall, with only enough space for a door leading into the dining room at one end. To get food from the tree-shaded pantry on the cold north side of the house, one had to cross the dining room many times a day.

Nine-foot ceilings throughout the downstairs rooms were such a waste of heat.

A wooden icebox lined with galvanized tin sat on the porch, in the shade. A compartment on top was for ice. As it melted, the water ran through a tube into a tray underneath. If that tray were not emptied periodically, it ran over onto the floor. Racks and shelves for the food were much like modern refrigerators. There was no crisper or freezer space.

I recall Dad cutting ice from the Racket Brook Inn pond, for the icehouse at the Dew Drop. Max always helped. With a long-handled chisel and the axe, they cut a hole in the ice large enough to accommodate the saw. Square blocks about 14 inches to 16 inches deep were cut, pulled out of the water with hand ice-tongs, and slid up a plank onto the handmade sleigh. It took a team of workhorses to pull the loaded sleigh up the mile- and a-half long hill to the Inn.

Since there was no icehouse at the farm, we never used the icebox. Perishables were kept in the pantry. The only ones we had were dairy products: milk, buttermilk, butter, Dutch cheese. Anything else was used up quickly or preserved.

Grandma's kitchen woodstove, inherited by Mother, sat out over two feet from the wall, taking up much space in the room. The cooking surface was approximately 20 inches by 24 inches with a reservoir at the right end, where hot water was always available. Food was cooked in pans on the griddles over the firebox to the left, and then moved to the surface between that and the reservoir to keep warm. The coffeepot and five-quart teakettle of hot water always setting on this surface were the sources of instant hot drinks: coffee, tea, or cocoa. An extra pot of coffee could be kept hot, but not boiling, on a swing-out metal shelf between the high warming oven over the top of the stove and the surface.

Extra food and serving dishes in cold weather were kept hot in the warming oven. In addition to setting bread dough to rise on top of it, chicken feathers, spread thinly on newspaper, were sometimes dried up there for pillows. In wintertime the area became the dry-kiln for wet mittens and gloves.

The baking oven was located beside the firebox, directly underneath the warming surface. Its thermometer was broken, but Mother judged by just sticking her hand inside if the heat were right, for whatever she was going to bake. To control that oven temperature with a wood fire was a chore of itself.

To put one stick or two, green or dry wood, or leave the red hot coals in the firebox alone until the food was done was a definite skill.

The last, but not least parts of the cook stove, were the ash-pit under the firebox and the draft controls. A hinged door on the firebox, with draft holes that could be adjusted to size by a sliding plate, controlled the amount of air let through it. A damper in the first length of stovepipe was set in sync with the draft control to keep the fire burning steadily and to keep heat from escaping. If the damper were set too tightly, smoke poured out into the room. An overfull ash-pit created draft control problems which also caused smoke. A smoking stove was especially disheartening to Mother when the walls had been newly papered or curtains freshly laundered. Ceiling wallpaper was always white to reflect the kerosene lamp light. Smoke dulled its luster, thus reducing its effectiveness.

Cleaning out the ash-pit was not as simple a job as one might think. The ashes were powder dry, but could have a live coal hidden in them. They were removed with a square-tipped, short-handled shovel and placed in a waste bucket or multipurpose coal hod. If not carefully lowered, they flew through the air as though windblown, covering everything with an ashen dust creating more work to remove. In keeping with the recycling era of the Great Depression, the ashes were not only used to cover the excrement under the outhouse, but were also spread over the garden to enrich the soil. Mixed with water to form a lye paste, the resulting product was effective in dissolving layers of hard, baked-on grease on the pancake griddle, or were used in making soap. In wintertime we scattered them over the ice, for a non-slip surface or to create friction under a spinning tire.

Should the game warden be seen approaching, a generous portion of sugar or coffee grounds sprinkled on a hot griddle to smolder killed the scent of illegal venison cooking. Venison has a unique cooking smell, unmistakable to anyone who is familiar with it.

All of the uses of the kitchen woodstove, including as a source of heat, were absolutely delightful in the wintertime. But having to use it all summer when the outside temperature might be 70 degrees was one not-so-good aspect of the Good Old Days.

The area behind the stove was not wasted space. It was the location of the woodbox, above which were hooks for outdoor wear. Over a period of time pieces of bark and sand, moistened from melting snow or ice on the wood, accumulated in the box, perhaps with carelessly discarded empty tobacco or cigarette packages. All needed to be cleaned out which was part of spring housecleaning. The box was taken outside, emptied, swept out, and set in the sun to dry.

One spring day when Verne and I had carried the woodbox from the Inn kitchen, onto the privy porch to empty it off the side, a coal-black fisher with a tail as long as its body darted out from underneath the porch.

*I*t certainly was easy to commune with nature in the primitive setting of my father's maple syrup production. Like so many others we knew, Dad was not motivated to do anymore manually than what was necessary to get a job done. Some folks called it lazy, but for him it was the height of efficiency.

"Why are you sitting there?" Mother asked in exasperation, many times when work was waiting.

"I'm thinking," he would reply, and he was—about how to perform the task with the least amount of exertion.

With the advent of spring came the making of maple syrup. A ring of bare ground around the maple trees meant that it was time to tap them. The revitalizing sap would be running, and could be harvested for maple syrup and related products.

When grandpa was living, he reserved a small grove of sugar maples in the *back forty,* but because of their proximity to the house, Dad had cut them down for firewood. He chose to tap the big trees in the front yard, and along Cleveland Road. It was easier there for Dan to pull the wagon that the barrel to hold the collected sap sat on.

From maple sap to maple syrup involved harder work in the olden days. Using a hand-operated auger, Dad bored holes in each tree to accommodate

Dad holds the reins; Dan pulls the wagon holding barrel of collected sap.

one or more sap spouts, depending on the size of the tree. On a hook which was slipped over the spout before inserting it into the tree, a bucket was hung to catch the dripping sap.

Over the years spur of the moment use of grandpa's bona-fide sap buckets had depleted their number. With little thought to the future, it was easy to just grab one to be nailed on the inside of the manger for a ration of oats alongside Dan's hay for instance, or for any other suitable purpose. Thus, along with the few remaining buckets an assortment of tin-pails were hung on the spouts.

Sap filled the containers at a speed dependent on the weather. An overnight frost followed by a sunny day created a more abundant run than continual cold temperatures.

Frequency of gathering the sap was based on this, but usually once a day.

Mother and Dad tend the Rube Goldberg setup for production of maple syrup.

Dad's idea of a sugarhouse was the great outdoors, recognizable only by the evaporating pan emitting steam from where it sat on a barrel-fireplace, salvaged from the remnants of grandpa's time. The stovepipe on the back created a draft for a steadily burning fire. Fieldstone stabilized the Rube Goldberg setup, and held the big bowl from grandma's old cream-separator from which sap flowed into the pan by opening a spigot at the bottom. Propped up with a board, the side or floor of a demolished outbuilding served as a windbreak. Talk about recycling!

The sap drawn back to this area was transferred from the barrel to the bowl, then at intervals to the evaporating pan. If a dead leaf or loose piece of bark from an overhanging branch fell into either of these, no one thought about pollution. It was simply removed when the foam that formed from the boiling process was taken off with a skimmer. The foam was considered an impurity that could taint the flavor and color of the syrup.

When the sap was reduced to a consistency ready to be drained into a smaller pan to finish thickening, Mother took over. Because the last whiffs of steam had been found to loosen the wallpaper when using the kitchen stove, this last process was done on a three-burner oil stove in the woodshed.

The syrup had to be watched carefully at this stage to be kept from boiling over. When the proper thickness was reached it was stored in glass jars for winter use. Mother's determination of this point was calculated by the rate at which it flowed from a spoon held in midair. If a candy thermometer were available, she didn't know about it.

Cooked longer, as with fudge, the syrup resulted in a soft, maple sugar when stirred. Stored in earthenware crocks, it was a delicious spread on warm, baking-powder biscuits or pancakes. Even hard maple candies could be produced by further cooking.

The season ended with the making of Jack Wax (commonly referred to as sugar on snow) from the remaining syrup left below the drain in the evaporating pan. Boiled until a spoonful of the syrup hardened into a taffy-like substance when spread across snow packed in a shallow pan, it could be easily rolled into a ball with a fork. Likened to a Big Daddy caramel sucker on a stick, it was a yummy treat.

Dad scrounges wood for the day.

While many men were taking advantage of the still frozen ground and bare hardwood trees to get up next season's firewood, Dad scrounged for the day. Much to Mother's chagrin, he was not one to seasonally fill the home woodshed. He was proud of the 30 full-cords he sold every year to Max Burns, co-owner of the garage and gas station in North River. But why stockpile what was always available for himself was Dad's way of thinking.

Verne had finished his time with the CCC and married Ruth Ann Durking, daughter of Hosea and Cora (Hunt) Durking of Indian Lake. I became Dad's *right hand man.*

Getting a tree from woodlot to woodstove was a slow process in the early Twentieth Century, especially in wintertime. Dan was harnessed and the skidding chain hooked to the whippletree behind him. With a cluck of the tongue and a giddy ap, reinforced with an occasional gee (right) or haw (left) by Dad, he was guided to the woodlot. Most times he simply walked along with no further encouragement or directions, for he was accustomed to the routine.

Dad and Dan in skidding-harness, on way to woodlot.

Dad carried a crosscut saw and an axe. A sledge hammer and a heavy iron wedge were also needed, and sometimes fastened to the harness on Dan's back or carried in a pack-basket with other simple tools, such as: pliers, a saw set used to adjust the teeth of the saw, and a saw gauge used with the file—to be sure the teeth were ground down evenly. It was better to have this done beforehand, but sometimes modifications had to be made while at the woodlot.

Once at the lot, a tree was selected and Dad chopped a notch into the side of it in which direction he wished it to fall. Then if he were alone, he removed one handle of the saw for balance and began to cut the tree on the opposite side. It was easier with a two-person operation. That's where I came in.

The saw had to be held perfectly straight across the cut with the teeth just touching the tree, not forced into it. If the saw teeth were sharp and set to specifications, they ate their way through quickly with little effort.

"Pick up your feet! Don't ride on the saw!" Dad instructed me. With a few of his orders, I finally got the *hang of it*.

Sometimes the tree would shift as it was cut, binding the saw. Then the wedge was driven into the cut to widen the space. With a few more long, even strokes of the saw, the tree fell with a resounding thud. Dan, tethered well out of harm's way, never flinched. He was used to all the sounds of wood cutting.

Dad limbed the fallen tree with the axe, leaving a 30-foot (or longer) log. I put any part of the limbs big enough for firewood aside to be bundled and picked up later, and I piled the remainder neatly in a depression on the ground where they were most obscure. In time they would help to level the area.

Dan was backed up to the butt of the tree, where the skidding chain was secured with a heavy iron hook. It didn't take long for him to drag the limbed tree to the house. Again, he needed little guidance, even to stop at designated places for a rest after a hard pull up an incline. Once at the house, he automatically stopped beside the circular saw rig.

Since sawing the tree into chunks was a separate task, it was more practical to cut and skid several trees one day and saw them into chunks on another, but Dad was seldom methodical. Dan was taken back to the barn, offered a drink at the watering barrel, led inside, and unharnessed.

We didn't need aerobic equipment or to do calisthenics. Activity such as this toned all our muscles.

The tree that had been skidded from the woodlot to the vicinity of the woodshed had to be cut into lengths convenient for one or two persons to lift onto the table of the buzz saw. A buzz saw revolved on a spindle, the other end of which formed a hub. A circular, canvas belt placed on the hub, crossed to prevent slipping off, and then stretched over the hub of a jacked-up, rear car wheel, mechanically operated the saw. I don't pretend to understand the dynamics of this, but with the car parked and motor running, the belt rotated causing the saw to turn. When the log on the saw table was pushed into the revolving saw, a chunk of any length could be cut.

One person could work alone, but again it was easier with two. My job was to help lift the log onto the table of the buzz saw, run to the other end to catch the stove length chunk, and toss it aside to keep the pile from building up under the saw. This procedure was referred to as *taking away*.

The chunks were then split into smaller pieces for the stoves. The size of the pieces was determined by whether they were to be used in the cook stove or the main heater in the parlor. With one chunk lying on the ground horizontally and a second one propped upright at an angle against it, Dad held it in place with his foot. With the axe aimed at the same angle, a single blow usually split that chunk with a sharp pop, the axe glancing harmlessly to the side or up against the base chunk. It was a real knack to know at what angle and with how much strength one should wield the axe. My part of the process ended by filling the woodboxes in the house, and keeping the ash-pits clean once the wood was consumed.

I was never allowed to handle the axe, not because the task required a lot of muscle or that it was dangerous, but because I was a girl. But Mother sometimes found herself setting a chunk on end and dealing it a smashing blow with the axe, when Dad didn't get around to plan far enough ahead.

I recall only one family accident when splitting wood that required a doctor. It happened to Verne in the forest. The axe struck a knot in a chunk, causing it to glance sideways through his boot into his foot. He limped to the house, where Mother helped to remove his footwear. Blood spurted from the wound. She instructed him to lie on his back on the porch and elevate his foot to the railing while waiting for Dr. Carrol.

When it was planting time the garden for small vegetables was plowed and spread over with a fertilizing layer of winter barn manure which was harrowed in with the drag. The drag was a piece of farm machinery equipped with spring-teeth and pulled by Dan. According to folklore, *spring snow storms were a poor man's fertilizer.*

After the *frogs had frozen up three times* indicating there would be no more frosts, and the moon's position was right, the tomato and cabbage plants started inside weeks before were put in. Other seeds were planted in long rows, with the cucumber hills set apart at the edge of the garden.

From now on Mother weeded and did most of the hoeing. I remember that when the cabbage plants began to head up, she bent down the loose, outside leaves every morning before sunup, and sprinkled the entire plant with a mild solution of salt water.

"Prevents worms," she said.

One year a piece of new ground needed to be broken for potatoes and corn. Dad hitched Dan to the plow, tied the reins together, slipped them over his shoulders (a dangerous practice commonly done by all farmers), and guided Dan through the field. After plowing, the sod was broken up and rocks were exposed with the drag. When the sods were as free of topsoil as possible, it was my job to toss them and the rocks onto the stone boat (a flat-bottomed transport made of heavy planks, fastened together with a mini-rim around all sides) to be pulled to an outside corner of the field by Dan.

The manure was harrowed in, and rows for planting were made with the plow and horse. It was difficult to guide the horse and hold the plow to make straight rows in green sod so I was to lead Dan by the bridle. Being short of stature I would practically be lifted off my feet when he swished his big head to ward off the flies around his ears. This resulted in a curve in the row.

"Dammit! Can't you keep that horse straight?" Dad yelled in exasperation.

"No, I can't!" I snapped back, equally as frustrated and simultaneously quaking in my shoes, for one never—but never—answered a parent back in that tone of voice those days.

"Well then, get on his back," Dad commanded, as he came around Dan's side to give me a boost.

The plot was finally ready for planting, but as far as the rows being straight, there was something left to be desired.

A big, summer chore on the farm was haying. Dad made only one cutting about midsummer. Because much of the land was rocky, lots of it was done by hand with a scythe and snath. I can see Dad in the field now sharpening the scythe with a whetstone. Standing the snath upside down, scythe extending about two and a half feet out, he held it with his left hand and passed the whetstone along alternate cutting edges of the scythe in quick even strokes with the right. *Swish-swash, swish-swash*. The continuous rhythm of the whetstone, from back to front of the scythe, left a razor-sharp cutting edge.

With skillful handling, he moved the scythe in even swings through the tall grass to lay down a straight row of hay to dry in the sun.

Dan pulled the two wheeled mowing machine with a long cutter-bar on the side over the open meadows. Dad, perched on the seat of the machine, guided Dan with one hand, and operated a handle that could raise and lower the bar over obstacles with the other.

After a day in the hot sun the cutting was turned over and shook out to dry through. This was a hand operation done with a pitchfork. If there were no rain, the hay was ready for the loft in two or three days. Inclement weather could prolong this process for as much as a week.

When the hay was dried to a golden brown it was ready to be raked. Dad hitched Dan to the hay-rake, another piece of farm machinery on wheels. It had a higher seat than the mowing machine and was equipped with long spring-teeth that could gather the hay into thick windrows left in place by operating a handle to lift the teeth off the ground. Then the rows were separated at intervals and piled into haycocks for convenient loading onto the farm wagon. The pitchfork and wooden hay-rake were the tools for this job.

To rake the hay and get it into the mow required a hot sunny day, all day long, sometimes into the evening hours. Dad pitched the hay onto the wagon with the fork, while Dan patiently stood still at each haycock. One of my jobs was to move the hay around on the wagon to even out the load. Another was to rake after Dad to clean up the last wisps of hay left on the ground. It was quite a trick to scoop these last rakings onto the wide hay-rake and gingerly lay them up on the load.

131

One day as I stood in the shade of the hay load before it was moved along, I felt a sting on my leg. I stomped my foot hoping to scare off a bee. Immediately, my leg felt as though it were on fire. I was standing on a hill of red ants. I dashed to the house for relief. Mother applied a paste made of baking-soda and water.

Resuming work, sweat poured down our foreheads into our eyes. Our throats would be parched from the heat. What a relief to get a cold drink from the bubbling spring at the edge of the meadow. A jug of vinegar switchel that Mother made that morning also quenched our thirst. Dad had carried it into the field earlier and set it in the spring to stay cold. It was a combination of vinegar, ginger, sugar, molasses, and water. I didn't care for it, but I would sneak a swig of Dad's Irish Cream Ale if he had some there.

He usually took a break then to have a few puffs of his pipe, laying it on a rock to cool when we went back to work. Later when we were far from the spring into the meadow, he often sent me back to get it. I hated the smell of tobacco and abhorred touching it, so picked it up wrapped in a big, burdock leaf to carry.

When the hay load was as high as possible to transport, Dan drew it to the barn. Riding on top was the fun part of the day's work.

The hay was pitched off the wagon as it was pitched on—with the fork. Dad tossed it overhead into the haymow opening and I mowed (pronounced *m · ŏw · ed*) it away, meaning to move it from the loft opening to the back of the storage area.

Not to disturb the black hornet's nest in the peak of the roof was always on my mind. By the time the job was finished, it had been a very long day.

When temperatures fell, leaves covered the ground, and nights were longer than days, my parents wondered how they were going to make ends meet financially all winter.

After the harvest was gathered, the choicest of it was sold by the bushel to the business people in North Creek: Dr. William Lee, a retired physician; Charlie Sullivan, the owner of a large grocery store; and Warren Ratcliff, a local attorney, each of whom had no time or chose not, to plant a garden. The income helped to pay the school taxes, and to buy a barrel of kerosene, for use in the oil lamps and to start the wood fires.

The harvest was gathered for sale: potatoes, carrots, and beets.

Dad drawed off one-gallon of kerosene at a time from the barrel into a can kept under the kitchen sink for those purposes. The screw cap for the spout had been lost, so he jammed a small potato over it.

Although there was plenty of home-preserved food and the barns were filled with hay, the chickens and livestock needed boughten grain. Dan had to have extra oats when he was worked hard getting up pulp and firewood.

As much a part of the fall harvest was the butchering. We always raised a pig—the only source of meat other than wild game throughout the winter. The piglet born in the spring had grown to a full-size porker by fall. Swill made up of cornmeal

133

and middlins, small or damaged apples, and vegetables unfit for winter storage was mixed with water to fatten it for slaughter. I do not remember if this concoction were always cooked, but it smelled appetizing enough for human consumption. It was collected in a huge, cast-iron kettle.

On butchering day, that kettle full of boiling water sat on a makeshift stone fireplace. Max came early to assist. Dad thought it more humane to use a gun rather than a knife for the slaughter. After the head and entrails were disposed of, the carcass was submerged in the boiling water to soften the bristles to be scraped off. It was then carved into various cuts, most of which were packed into five-gallon jars of smoked salt. The fat was *tried out* (rendered), strained, and poured into small containers to harden as lard.

From bacon came the most diversified product of pork: grease. Bacon grease was used for everything from baking to a sandwich spread, a topping for mashed potatoes or pancakes, shortening for fried foods, and even provided one ingredient of handmade soap. Dad dipped nails in bacon grease to prevent wood from splitting when building.

A Thanksgiving story from my paternal grandparent's lives emphasizes the importance of bacon grease as a food:

The women were busy all morning in the kitchen. They vowed that this was one meal when none of them would have to get up for something once all were seated. With that in mind, the table was laden with condiments: perhaps spiced crab apples, apple sauce, and mustard pickles.

Roast pork complete with scorch gravy, mashed potatoes, and a vegetable was ready. Homemade bread, maybe baking-powder biscuits or johnny cake, made for an exceptionally bountiful meal. If turkeys were available at the general store, they would have been considered a luxury beyond my family's reach, as would have been raising one.

I never heard of a hunter that saw one in the wilds at that time.

Salads, fruit other than apples, fresh vegetables, or more than one hot vegetable was not an option. But on the sideboard were apple and mince pies, venison the main ingredient of the mincemeat.

During the meal preparation, other family members arrived. Due to distances, lack of transportation, and the weather, the Thanksgiving meal might be the only family gathering of the year.

"Come and get it!" announced an impatient young voice.

Grandpa took his place at the head of the table. Little ones squabbled over who would sit beside him. The womenfolk poured the coffee and milk, asked if there were anything anyone else wanted, and sat down, confident that there was nothing else anyone could possibly want.

"Was there any of that fresh bacon grease left over from breakfast?" grandpa, surveying the table from one end to the other, asked in a demanding voice.

Wonder if the stage has gone through yet? The question referred to daily mail delivery which we looked forward to as eagerly as we looked forward to daily meals. It was almost our only connection to the outside world. There was no greater distance between experiencing a high or a low, than receiving or not receiving a letter from someone.

The shortcut to the main highway made it more convenient to locate the mailbox there, than to place it at the end of Cleveland Road. Although delivery was made by truck, it was still referred to as the stage. Jay Goodspeed, the carrier for our route, continued to allow people to ride.

No telephone, no radio, TV only somewhere on a drawing board, the nearest neighbor a half-mile away; these were all reasons that increased our dependence on the daily mail for communication. Letters from distant relatives and friends, with news that had become history by the time we read of it, were welcome anyhow.

Junk mail, although much less of it then than now, and the seasonal "wish books" (the *Sears Roebuck* and *Montgomery Ward* catalogs) were the way we discovered what was new in manufacturing and style. The only thing I remember my family ordering was footwear. We couldn't afford anything else. But sometimes we got an idea of how to make a reasonable facsimile. Seed catalogs in the spring brought high hopes for new growth and productive days after a long, dreary winter.

When, as a writing lesson, the high school English class was encouraged to write to the boys in Service during World War II, girls especially needed no further prompting to do so. I continued the correspondence to the end of the war. I was so thrilled with my first V-mail letter from a soldier. His handwritten pages from Europe had been censored, and the writing condensed onto a stiff paper less than the size of a postcard before it was sent on to me.

What a shock it was to receive inquiries from former sportsmen who had stayed at the Inn, asking if the service were to be continued at the farm. My parents had never even considered it. But former guests were so insistent they decided to accommodate hunters only who were willing to forsake the comforts of their city homes to vacation in excellent Adirondack hunting country. They came of their own accord, with no more concern for their health and safety than what had been shown them at the Inn.

With continuation of the business came additional activity for me. I inherited yet another one of Verne's jobs: to help Dad with the guiding. I had shared many woodland adventures with him, one of the first, when I was 12-years-old.

I had heard the signal shots of a lost hunter which were: two sharp cracks in succession, a pause followed by a single shot—two sharp cracks in succession, a pause followed by a single shot, etc . . . . The sounds came from behind Prear Pond, which was dense with undergrowth and the location where it frequently happened, even to Verne once.

Dad, with his new gun and well-filled cartridge belt (gifts from grateful hunters), and author team-up as guides.

"Let's go find him," Dad immediately said, when I told him what I had heard, taking me along in the usual capacity of being able to hear well. He knew the area, and was reasonably sure that the sounds would not be distorted by echoes from distant mountains or ledges.

As we made our way through the brush calling out "HELLO" from time to time, the bushes ahead of us parted revealing a half-grown bear. I sprung into Dad's arms as though bounced off a trampoline. He staggered, but remained erect. Scared from behind by the lost person and running into us in front, the bear, with a little grunt, pivoted and ran-off at a 90-degree angle through the woods. With hind legs springing between front ones, he seemed to roll along over rocks and logs like a big, black fur ball.

Dad guffawed as he helped me regain my footing, and told me that the animal was probably as startled by me as I had been by him. I did not appreciate his sense of humor.

"But had it been a cub, the mother bear might have been dangerously near," he said.

Verne with the bear he bagged behind Prear Pond.

We soon found the lost person. Some years later, Verne killed a mature bear weighing over 350 pounds in the same vicinity.

Shortly after the incident with the bear, Dad taught me how to handle a gun and hunt. In my youth I bagged my fair share of squirrels and predators. But on my first venture as Dad's guiding partner, I realized I would never become a serious hunter.

We had taken a hunting party into the woods on Buck Hill, near the Dew Drop Inn. After Dad placed the hunters on watches, he circled back and began yipping like a dog. Traveling parallel with him, but some distance away, I gave out my best "ow-o-o-o" hoping it sounded like a baying hound. Imagine my astonishment when coming face to face with a deer probably frightened toward me by Dad! It never occurred to me to scare her toward the watching hunters or to shoot. I just stared in amazement at her as she stared back at me, before she suddenly bounded away.

On one deer hunt, I witnessed a once-in-a-lifetime scene of a partridge standing on a log to drum with its pulsing, nonstop wings. The loud, rhythmic sound to a staccato beat was highly exciting to me.

A week's deer-take at the farm.

But the most memorable happening was the story never told. One season a hunter who had vacationed with us for years was accompanied by his brother, a non-hunter who came just for the experience. Dad and I took them out behind the farm, where there were several small ridges between Hooper's Pond, and Davis Mountain. We had made a couple of short drives and having seen nothing, were still-hunting our way back to the house. We planned to go to a different location after lunch.

Totally surprising was the sight of a beautiful buck standing on a distant ridge, its big set of horns silhouetted against the sky. Dad, in the lead, had the clearest view through the trees. He raised his hunting rifle to his shoulder, sighted the animal in, finger on the trigger. Then, the observing gentleman, in his excitement, stepped right in front of the gun. Dad immediately dropped both his arms to his sides, his entire body seeming to droop forward like a wilting flower.

The moment was so tense, not a sound was made by anyone. Taking a deep breath, Dad simply stepped forward to resume the walk toward home, the rest of us following in utter silence. Of all the hunting tales he told, I never once heard him mention this incident.

By only word of mouth business expanded and letters from new hunters asking for reservations filled our mailbox.

*E*ven though accommodating hunters brought in sufficient extra money for daily living expenses, more was needed for the property taxes due in January. When at the Inn, some of the hunters had asked to buy a Christmas tree to take back home to the city. Living at the farm now, Dad saw a way to earn that extra money. From his many woodland acres he cut several evergreen trees to sell, making a successful business venture.

I don't know what he charged. But with bread $ .10 a loaf and gasoline $ .20 a gallon, I am sure his price was proportionate. It was probably no more than $ 1.00 each, regardless of size.

We hear a naturally grown Christmas tree commonly referred to as a Pine, and all cones spoken of as Pinecones. The truth of the matter is that our Spruce, with its thick branches, and the fragrant Balsams, including their cones, were far superior as Christmas trees. A hardened, chewy substance on the bark of the Spruce was also a satisfactory form of chewing gum. But the blisters full of sticky pitch on the Balsam bark were a nuisance to say the least. Dad never sold the flimsy White Pines for Christmas trees. We had no other evergreens.

There were no tree farms, or standard ways of pruning to form a nicely shaped tree. Thinning the groves was the best way to help a tree grow uniformly. I claimed the first one unfit for sale as our own, and nailed a couple of boards crosswise to the bottom for a stand. The unattractive side was placed near the wall, preferably in a corner. We never thought to set it in water to keep the needles fresh. As the harvesting began early, it is only fair to say that more than one, poorly-shaped tree, was replaced by another when all the needles dried and fell off before the holiday.

My great-Uncle Bernard Beakbane's brother, Lionel, contacted us. He was from the Fernwood Fish Hatchery, in South Glens Falls, and wanted a truckload of evergreen trees, together with cone-laden boughs. The latter were used for window-boxes and wreathes he told us. He remained our biggest customer for years. The thickest clusters of cones are at the top of mature trees over forty feet tall, so Dad cut the big trees for the top branches and sold the rest of the tree as pulp wood.

One of our buyers showed us how to fashion a wreath by using heavy wire bent into a circle for a frame with fastened sprigs of evergreen placed on one side. We had only coarse thread left over from the store inventory to fasten with. This was not very satisfactory as the sprigs slipped and slid from our grasp and the finished product was thin. We finally mastered the art enough for our own decorative pleasure. A few cones, strategically placed, did make the wreaths more attractive when hung over a nail. The task was much easier when through someone else's cleverness a bent coathanger made a sturdier frame with a perfect hook for hanging.

*T*here were few ways for teenage farm girls to earn money. The word allowance, in terms of money for children, would have been outlandish. The much-in-demand for childcare in this day, was not a concept in the mid-Twentieth Century. Mothers were always at home. If there were a need for them to be elsewhere, children were taken along, even to weddings or funerals.

But I needed more mature and lucrative work than gathering scrap iron and picking wild berries for sale, or doing some jobs that had been Verne's such as disposing of unwanted barn cats for a neighbor. Digging fish worms, and catching frogs or crawfish for Max's bait shop was also unappealing to me.

A federally funded program, the National Youth Association (NYA), provided eligible school students with a small stipend to work either as a teacher-aide, or in the cafeteria preparing pea soup or hot cocoa for the students. The money made a big difference in being able to purchase needed school items such as a piece of sports equipment, or in my case—music books.

Cocoa and pea soup are foods easily scorched. Few of us who worked in the kitchen were tall enough to reach the bottom of the huge cauldrons to stir the contents. Being a coed group of workers, I must say we weren't always concentrating on cooking either. When the other students marched in for lunch, they knew by the disgusting smell that the hot food would be less than appetizing many days.

Beecher Smith, a lone chicken farmer, who was known by my parents and lived within walking distance of our home, offered me a job of tidying up his house one day a week when he went into town on business. I welcomed the opportunity.

Housework I knew, and knew well. My pay would be $ 1.00. I arrived at his home, punctually, Saturday morning. He familiarized me with the place, left instructions for me to gather the eggs, separating the cracked and unclean ones, and put them in the pantry when finished with the cleaning. Then he left for the day.

I noticed there were breakfast dishes in the sink: a coffee cup, silverware, and a small plate with evidence that eggs had been eaten. What but, for a chicken farmer? A small, black, iron frying-pan sat on the stove. *I'll wash those few dishes later.* I went upstairs to do the chamber work.

His house was modern compared to ours with adequate, up to date cleaning supplies. *This job is a cinch.* I went about to change the bed linens, dust the furniture, and dust mop the hardwood floors and stairs. The parlor and dining room were easily neatened also, as was the kitchen. Then I mopped all the floors with a rag mop and wiped down the stairs. *Now to wash those breakfast dishes, tend the chickens, and leave.*

Putting the dishes in the dish pan, I filled the same with hot water from the teakettle setting on the woodstove. When I reached for some dish soap on the shelf under the enclosed kitchen sink—surprise! Stacked there were the dirty dishes of the entire week. It was obvious that eggs had been eaten at nearly every meal. Thereafter, the first thing I did after entering his home, was to put all those dishes in the sink to soak, while I cleaned through. Once a routine was established, it was a most satisfying first job away from home.

When my employer decided to replace his battery-powered, tabletop Philco radio, he offered it to me in exchange for two Saturdays worth of work. My parents were delighted to find it under the Christmas tree that year, 1940.

*O*ther than the fact that Christmas vacation was over and school was about to start again, New Year's Eve was just another night in our life. One year a freezing rain, all afternoon, had coated everything with a layer of ice. By early evening it had subsided and a light wind came up. As a bright, nearly-full moon and millions of stars broke through, the sparkling landscape was truly a winter wonderland. Under the weight of the ice, small tree branches began to snap with reverberating sounds resembling the clink of crystal, champagne glasses being raised in a toast.

Mother on short-cut path to mailbox in aftermath of ice-storm.

Ice storms did not wreak the havoc to mankind that they do today. There were no electric power or phone lines where I lived. Our main concern was whether the old outbuildings would hold up under the weight of the ice, or if damage would occur to the apple trees and sugar maples.

I was trying to stay erect while carrying the barn lantern on the way to the barn, to help bed down the animals for the night. I wondered how well I could see inside the building, for keeping the lighted lantern level was impossible when slipping and sliding on the path. This caused the flame to flare upward and smoke up the chimney. I had tried to wipe it clean with a crumpled newspaper before leaving the house, having lit the lantern there for safety sake.

Early next morning, I was out sprinkling the paths to the outbuildings with wood ashes. I carried my Brownie box camera, purchased with money earned at the chicken farm, and took some photos.

When the sun replaced a fading moon, the prime example of beauty and the beast was spectacular—the beast being the power of an ice storm to cause destruction. Beautiful were the mounds of ice covered low bushes, forming a glistening, igloo village in the back yard. A glittering background of trees on the mountainside reflected the sun's rays. In sharp contrast were the apple trees opposite. Although the ice covered branches shone, the trees appeared to be in mourning over the loss of broken limbs scattered on the ground. If this were

Ice-encased apple tree limbs appear to be in state of mourning.

Mother Nature's way of pruning (as someone else had once written), she certainly did a good job.

In the event of a snowstorm thereafter, snowplows with heavy chains on the tires cleared the roads. In the bitter wind, two men, standing on the back of a slightly elevated dumptruck-bed, worked in unison to alternately spread shovels full of sand in a crisscross pattern on the road. Side roads were not sanded.

There were five hills, some fairly steep, between my home and the school. I never knew of an accident. This was certainly proof of the skills of road maintenance crews and schoolbus drivers.

School was still in holiday recess, so after the storm I helped Dad replenish our dwindling supply of firewood. He tapped sharp metal corks into Dan's shoes, and we took him in his skidding harness along Cleveland Road to get a tree from the pasture land. Reins wrapped loosely around my hands, I held him at some distance, while Dad stepped over the snowbank to cut a tree that hung dangerously over the narrow road.

With a sharp crack, an ice encased, dead limb high above fell through the air and hit Dan on the rump. Bolting in fright, he leaped forward tightening the reins on my hands and yanking me off my feet.

"Whoa! Whoa boy!" Dad yelled.

Dan was spooked, taking off at a dead run. I could not let go of the reins, and my body slid along the hard-packed icy road like a toboggan.

"Whoa! Whoa boy! Whoa!" I, too, yelled at the top of my lungs to no avail.

All to once (a common phrase much used by old-time Adirondack story tellers) my body slammed up against a huge, solidly packed ball of snow that had rolled back into

145

the road after the snowplow went through. Clad in layers of winter clothing and possessing the resiliency of youth, I was not hurt on impact. But the sharp jerk of the reins on the bit in Dan's mouth was just enough to bring him up short.

He had covered about 200 feet, but Dad caught up rather quickly. Speaking in a quiet voice while using a firm hand, he turned Dan around and guided him back to the half-sawed tree. Work proceeded with no further incident and the smooth, hard-packed, snow covered road made for easy skidding of the tree to the house.

Under a canopy of ice-laden tree limbs, the plow leaves Cleveland Road with hard-packed snow.

Survival during the Great Depression and World War II years promoted a deep faith in God, invoking His help with everything from providing good weather for a bountiful harvest to relieving the horrors of war.

When we lived at the store, Mother worked with the Ladies' Aid Society, and she and we children attended church services regularly. We were taught the children's prayer, *Now I Lay Me Down To Sleep*, as soon as we were able to talk. When we moved to the Inn, my parents, often without a car, lived their faith daily. Dad, like John Walton of the TV series, maintained there were other ways of being a good Christian than belonging to an organized church. Mother's help was requested for miles around, perhaps to act as a midwife or sit with a dying person. She never refused.

The farm was about three-miles from church. At age 15, I developed a thirst for religion and walked the distance. Mother insisted that appearance was important when visiting a house of God and we should dress our best. That best meant mostly everyday wear: freshly laundered, starched, and ironed. Silk stockings and a hat were gestures of respect.

My great-Aunt Olive Beakbane had brought me a new raincoat. It was made of a bright red, rustling fabric. One Sunday when the weather was cloudy, I wore it.

Returning home on Cleveland Road, I had to pass Arthur Cleveland's farm. Arthur had acres of fenced-in pasture land, the fence always in need of repair somewhere. He also had a large, breeding bull living there. I guess that animal was attracted to my new raincoat. He broke through the fence, snorted and pawed, and headed toward me. I removed the raincoat, threw it at him, and while he was investigating what it was I took to the woods, emerging at the top of the old, one-room schoolhouse hill. What a great relief when Willard Davis came along in his first car and gave me a ride home! My thirst for religion was quenched for awhile.

Mother emphasized acts of charity to be God's work, and now said I was old enough to share the neighbor's sorrows by attending funeral wakes. One of the first was for our closest neighbor, Ida Sanders. The deceased were kept at home for three days and nights, with a 24-hour vigil.

A room was cleared of furniture and the honored dead was laid out there. After the funeral, while others went on to the cemetery, a couple of people remained at the house to put the room back in order. I volunteered for that job along with another neighbor, Rose Williams, a tall, raw-boned lady. As we each took opposite ends of a daybed which served as a couch to move it back into place, my second step wedged my foot in a spittoon which had been concealed underneath. Spittoons were receptacles for tobacco juice and that one was full.

I also sat nights at the wake for Rose's mother, Gram Davis, as she was affectionately known. The outhouse at that residence was about 40 feet from the house at the edge of the woods. I was terrified to walk through the darkness, so sat many hours in agony until daylight. I wondered if attending wakes was a form of penance as much as a charitable act.

That was the year I had my first full-time job away from home. It was at Uncle Bucky's Racket Brook Inn, where his wife, Aunt Lutie, became a mentor to me. She was a person of great faith, and on the wall of the bedroom where I slept hung a tapestry of the Lord's Prayer. It offered a sense of security for a young girl on her first venture away from home, and I learned it verbatim.

Racket Brook Inn in its hey-day. Photo courtesy of Milda Burns Circa 1900's

*I*n the early 1900's Racket Brook Inn, had been a boarding house for men employed in the garnet mine, at the end of Casey Mountain. Stairs at each end of the building provided access to several bedrooms on the second floor. Five- or six-tables were in the dining room. Twenty- or-more guests could be seated.

There were only two-tables in the dining room of the Dew Drop Inn, and one of them was set up for only two people. Meals were served in shifts, family style with no choice of food. All that was required of a waitress was to keep plenty of it available.

At Racket Brook Inn, having a choice of desserts was a new experience for me. When I announced the different ones from the dining room doorway, imagine my confusion as voices came at me from all sides. Aunt Lutie quickly came to my aid with pad and pencil, and quietly explained that I should go to each table for the diner's order. Lesson Number One in the outside world! I learned a lot about the finer art of waitressing from Aunt Lutie.

My other duties included washing the dishes by hand, setting up the tables for breakfast after the supper hour, and laundering the day's dish towels and hanging them out to dry overnight. If silver needed polishing or the back stairs had to be wiped down those, too, were my responsibilities at the end of the day. In addition to room and board, I earned $ 5.00 a week.

Rose was the cook's helper. As she was icing a cake one day, a mischievous, little boy of one of the guests streaked through the kitchen. He paused just long enough to stick a finger into the center of the cake and run.

"If you do that again!" Rose, in her throaty voice, exclaimed, as she raised the spatula she was using and in long strides chased him. He could really run.

At the end of the season, she and I decided to reward ourselves with an adventure. The Trailways Bus had just established a brief stint of transportation in the vicinity. We would make a trip to Warrensburg, New York, 25 miles to the south, to visit her friends who conducted a greenhouse business there.

We caught the bus with the intention of returning on it that afternoon. Neither of us had a watch, and missed it. Luckily, a delivery of flowers had to be made to our area early next morning. The greenhouse driver said we could ride back home with him in his panel truck. That night, we shared a room at the Rice guest house—another new adventure.

Awakened at daybreak by birds singing outside, there was only one way to remotely discern what time it was.

"What time do birds start singing in the morning?" I asked Rose. Of course she didn't know either, but we dressed and went out curbside to wait for our ride.

From the incident, I recognized the need for a telephone in my parent's home, and used some of my summer wages to have one installed. It was connected to a party-line through a single system, linked to the main office called central. Each family called received a different signal distinguished by length of the rings. Two long rings might be for the Jones's family; three short ones for the Smith's; two longs, one short for someone else; etc . . . .

The rings sounded in all homes on the party-line. Soon every family recognized each other's signals, allowing anyone interested to eavesdrop, referred to as "rubbering in". If a person wished to call someone outside the party-line, a single ring notified central, where the connection was made by an operator.

That may have been the era when the three fastest ways of communication were known as *telegraph, telephone, or tell a woman*—apropos the party line.

Our phone was used sparingly. There was no idle chitchat between teenagers just for the sake of it, not even when I reached dating age.

My experience at Racket Brook Inn helped prepare me

for what I would be doing at Thirteenth Lake Lodge, where I was employed for three summers. The name reflected the beautiful lake, a short walk from the lodge in the hamlet of North River. Several cabins were located in the background.

Thirteenth Lake Lodge, where the author was employed for three summers.

Inside the lodge were many guest rooms, bathrooms, and a large dining room that could accommodate 40 or more people, an employee dining room, and a so-called men's room, where the hired men could relax and smoke before or after the dinner hour.

The business, owned by Mr. and Mrs. Ben Straight, also employed a cook, a cook's helper (my mother for a couple of years—her only outside-of-the-home job ever), a laundress or two, two chamber maids, and four waitresses of which I was one. Extra duties for us were to make side salads and to operate the electric dishwasher.

Employees were always served before the guests from the same menu. One specialty of the house was the strawberry shortcake. It was made up of their garden berries and homemade baking-powder biscuits. Topped with rich whipped cream from the lodge's own cow, plus a generous scoop of ice cream (having been made on the back porch in a hand cranked ice cream maker by one of the hired men), it was truly a favorite dessert of the guests.

Waitresses wore white uniforms and tea aprons until the day that my roommate took all the soiled laundry, including mine, to

her home. I had no uniform to wear in the dining room. All that might suffice was one of her blue-gingham, cotton dresses. I explained the situation to Mrs. Straight who always took her own meals in the guest dining room, perhaps to supervise our work. She gave me permission to wear it and liked the appearance so well, with the little, white apron, that she gave us all permission to wear our starched cotton frocks thereafter.

Waitresses at Thirteenth Lake Lodge: (left to right) L. Raymond, H. Maffuid, W. Farrell, and M. _____.

Occasionally, a picnic was held for the guests at a spot on the lake shore known as Elizabeth Point. We waitresses liked that, for it gave us extra time off in the afternoon. We worked seven-days a week, and the couple leisure hours each afternoon was collectively our day off. We were free to use the boats belonging to the lodge or go swimming. Sometimes we had our own picnic by the lake using veggies pilfered from the lodge garden, theorizing that we were doing a good deed by thinning them out.

One evening when my date and I were on an outing across the lake, enjoying some of those veggies with hot dogs, Charlie (the area teen prankster) unfastened our boat, thereby allowing it to float away from the shore. He didn't return it until dawn making it very difficult to explain to my coworkers why I was out all night.

Four of us girls shared a cabin with two bedrooms, a lavatory, and a small leisure-activity room. Showers and commodes were in a separate building. In addition to room and board, we made $ 10.00 a week, and had social security benefits.

*O*ne of the most traumatic experiences of my young life happened while I was in high school. About 4:00 A.M., one winter morning Mother woke me. She was suffering a nasal hemorrhage. Every rag, washcloth, and towel available was saturated with blood. Our family doctor, Dr. Carrol, had been assigned to military service. Dr. Beckry, an elderly retired physician, was filling in for him. I phoned his office and waited—and waited—and waited, growing more apprehensive by the moment.

With the second anguished call to the doctor's office, I was informed that he had come, but couldn't find the place.

"Get someone who knows the family to come with you. This woman needs a doctor!" a women on the party-line interrupted. It was Myrtle, a neighbor. Apparently, she had rubbered in on the first call too. To me she said, "I'll be right down." Party-lines had their good points.

She and the doctor arrived about the same time. After he had administered first-aid, Mother, knowing how much I hoped for perfect attendance at school, insisted that I ride back to town with him. Myrtle assured me that she would stay the day with her.

On returning home that night, I found a dark house, fires out, and the water frozen-up. I knew that regardless of what had transpired with Mother, the water situation had to be taken care of immediately. So, as I had seen Dad do, I lit the barn lantern and positioned it in the crawl-space under the kitchen floor, beneath the elbow of the water pipe. That was the most likely place for the water to be frozen.

Then I phoned Myrtle. She informed me that Mother's condition had not improved after Dr. Beckry left. Dad had taken her to Dr. Glenn's office in North Creek. A swirl of emotions raced around in my head. *How long had it taken Dad to get the car started?* The old Maxwell had long since been retired to the *back forty.* A Model A (or B) Ford had replaced it. Luckily, this was one of the winters that the license hadn't been cancelled. But it had not been started in weeks. The radiator needed to be filled with tepid water and the oil-pan warmed. *Did Dad have to put on chains? Did he get Mother to Dr. Glenn in time?*

Myrtle continued. Max, who lived near town was alerted, and following the doctor's advice, had driven Mother on to Glens Falls Hospital. With a much relieved feeling of her whereabouts, I noticed the water faucet had begun to drip and removed the lantern from underneath the pipe. I started the wood fires, banked them for the night, and turned in for a restless sleep. When I heard Dad's late arrival home, it was obvious that he had had *one too many* to calm his nerves, so I just left him alone to go to bed.

Next morning, after arising too early to call Max, I took care of the stoves, left a fresh pot of coffee, and went to school. Seeking permission to use the office phone to call him, he told me it had been determined that high blood pressure had caused Mother's nasal hemorrhage, which otherwise might have been a stroke. It was a condition that could lead to heart trouble, and a person must be conscious of that for life. She was to be discharged from the hospital the next day; he would bring her to his home to recuperate.

*M*y distant cousin, Elmer Raymond, and his wife, Ruth, were operating the McSweeny Hotel and Red Diner, in North Creek. They invited me to work for them, and finish high school locally. The opportunity to make some money, live in more comfort, and have a better social life was tempting. I did feel like a misfit in school where I was. I had only been on two field trips during my three-years in high school. One was with the girl's softball team, when a substitute was needed—the other, to participate in a band concert.

I don't remember who I rode with to the ball game, but the band members were transported by bus to the music event in Saratoga, New York. That trip resulted in a moment of embarrassment on arriving home late at night at the path leading to the farm. Dad had hung the barn lantern, with its smoke-streaked chimney, on a tree branch to light my way. By this time, most band members would have electric porch lights left on or parents waiting for them in the family car. *What would the kids on the bus think?*

Additionally, there were only half as many students in the class as had been in first grade when we started. One boy and myself were the only out-of-towners. When the others chatted about after-school fun such as swimming at the Drop Off in summer or skiing at Pig Hollow in winter, I experienced a momentary feeling of isolation. But I was needed for late afternoon chores at home, and conditioned to think the lifestyle of townsfolk could never be ours anyhow.

The farm was located on the Warren/Hamilton County line. My family were considered as Town of Indian Lake residents, and I attended Indian Lake Central School. But our address was North River. Anything we needed to buy had to be purchased in North Creek. I felt little connection to any place or anybody. However, I had been with the same classmates for 11 years, and wanted to be a part of their graduation. I declined my cousin's kind offer.

Lee and Pearl (Farrington) Raymond stand in front of guest's car. Circa 1941

Once resigned to life at the farm, my thoughts returned to the sojourn spent there after leaving the store. Like then, I really could be contented wherever Mom and Dad were.

Within a few-yards of the house along Cleveland Road, was the big, flat rock I used to set my dolls on while I picked a bunch of wild flowers for Mother. Flowers still grew in abundance there—violets, May flowers, adder tongues in spring, buttercups, daisies, black-eyed Susans later, all interspersed with a profusion of ferns. That rock didn't appear half as large to me as it had 10 years before. But it was plenty big enough to lay flat on my back and gaze at the cumulus clouds in the sky, for imagination to run wild. *Was it a ghostly dragon floating by or my Prince Charming on a white horse?* It was peaceful to feel, that in all likelihood, no car would pass to disturb my daydreams.

I had no desire to pick the flowers now; they were so beautiful waving in the breeze right where they were. Besides, Mother enjoyed grandma's patch of miniature white roses that could be seen and smelled through the open kitchen window.

To be awakened every morning by the robin's cheerful song in the Maple tree outside my bedroom window, or by the rooster's *cock a doodle doo* from the barnyard was such a homey way to start the day. Squawking, hungry hens emitted soft clucks when I sprinkled cracked-corn across their fenced-in yard. After slopping the oinking hog, she made contented grunts and snorts, while slobbering her snout back and forth in the trough for the swill. When she had cleaned up the last morsel, she edged up to the side of the pen for a bristly backrub, before settling down on her side in the mud.

All the senses were awakened here in this Adirondack environment. With the knowledge that this was my heritage, I finally recognized the farm to be a happy home, rather than a place as the store, and Inn, had been.

The author puts in a flower-bed, recognizing the farm to be a happy home.

*L*ike nearly every American my age, I remember exactly where I was on December 7, 1941, when Japan bombed Pearl Harbor. Mother and I were invited to ride around the horn with relatives. It was, and still is, a scenic drive through the lower Adirondacks. From North River, New York the road follows Route 28 north through several towns, to Route 28 N that one takes south to Route 28 once more, toward

North Creek. Turning on Route 28 north again in North Creek, brings one back to North River, completing the circle.

On a beautiful, unseasonably, warm day, we were just passing the rural cemetery outside the town of Newcomb, New York, when the music on the car radio was interrupted by the devastating news. Even though Max and Verne were both married with families, they were in the Selective Service Bill age range. With the war on both the Atlantic and Pacific fronts now, Mother immediately became concerned for them.

School students saved their pennies, nickels, and dimes to purchase war bonds. Classes competed for the honor of buying the most. A plane-spotter tower was erected on Crow Hill in Indian Lake. Mrs. Early, a thoughtful sixth-grade teacher who lived in town, invited me to stay at her house for my turn to watch. Participants were awarded an Army/Navy E pin. I again gathered scrap iron, this time for the war effort. Although the kerosene lights at my home only glimmered (one couldn't see their light from the barn to the house), my family felt a measure of pride by joining blackout practices.

As a senior, my school life changed for the better. Wilma, a Junior, befriended me and we became fast-friends. Her family lived nearer town and often invited me for sleepovers so that I could attend some of the evening events at school, such as the Halloween party and the Senior Ball. We both worked the next summer at Thirteenth Lake Lodge. She, nor any of our mutual friends, cared that I lived on a dirt road.

We rode back and forth to each other's homes, and sometimes to the village with the mail carrier. Boys often hitchhiked to meet us. With those lucky enough to have access to an automobile, we double dated (and triple dated) to pool gasoline ration tickets and save mileage on car tires. Our dates sometimes put pieces of worn out tires inside thin spots on other tires to protect inner-tubes. My class of 1943 forsook the senior trip to Washington D.C., donating the funds raised to the war effort. We published our own yearbook, contributing the monies it would have cost for professional publications, if it had indeed been available.

Not only lack of finances prevented my aspirations to become a nurse; the government had established a free Cadet Nurse's Program. But due to Mother's health problems at the time, I didn't want to commit to long-term study. Instead, I followed my great-Uncle Burke Cross's suggestion to board with him and Aunt Florence in Milford, Connecticut. There, opportunity for employment and trade-school was available, in nearby Bridgeport. I soon found a job as a bookkeeper with the Singer Manufacturing Company, which had been converted to a war plant producing the Sperry bomb sight. Employees earned the coveted Army/Navy E pin, making a second one for me. My wages were $ 18.00 a week, $ 5.00 of which I paid for room and board.

Evenings I attended Comptometer School. Before waiting for the result of my final exam in the course, I came back home to my beloved Adirondacks and found employment with National Lead Company at Tahawus, New York, as an Industrial Laboratory Technician, which had nothing to do with either nursing or comptometry.

*M*ost of the calendar holidays held little meaning for us. With no media of any kind in the home for years, and absence of commercial-hype as we know it now, they came and went much as any other day.

New Year's was just another day, past the excitement of Christmas, and too far from the bright days of spring.

Valentine's Day was fun in grade school, where the teacher had made a colorful mailbox to drop our class-made valentines in. Somewhere I saw an 8 inch by 10 inch, tissue paper valentine for adults with a picture of a young *swain* in a swallow tail suit and a pretty *flapper* girl. The caption read: "I love my wife, but OH you kid!"

St. Patrick's Day became meaningful to me only when it became my wedding day in 1946, to Ernest D. Warner, a co-worker (before he enlisted in the United States Army), and son of Curtis and Margaret (Blaise) Warner of North Creek.

April Fool's Day brought its merriment, in and out of school.

I knew the religious importance of Easter Sunday, but not in depth. Usually we had no means of transportation for church, and winter weather was still hanging on. Family history did record that a great-Aunt Lois Cross (in her teens) had dressed up in light-clothing for church one Easter Sunday, caught pneumonia, and died. The Easter bunny visited me only once, when my great-Aunt Olive happened to come at the same time.

In May, elementary students made colorful, paper mini-baskets for mothers, and we learned about children dancing around a May Pole in foreign lands. Every Decoration Day, as Memorial Day was then known, my family endeavored to take lilac bouquets, in a jar of water, to place on family graves in the cemetery.

I do not remember designated Mother's or Father's Days from my youth. But every day with Mom and Dad was significant for me. Just how significant deserves more than a few words.

"Just a housewife" was what my mom was, but every day was her day in my eyes. Being raised in an Adirondack tourist environment gave her some contact with the outside world, but also kept her home. Bringing up her own family in this same kind of environment meant that she was always there for me during my formative years. That is how best I remember her.

At the store, her constant awareness of where I was and what I was doing, plus her ability to appear as if by magic to my call of "Mamma!" She was always there.

When she made a peanut butter sandwich for Verne's school lunch pail (during my preschool days at the farm) she made one for me too, so I could play school with my dolls when he was gone. I dragged the rag doll around that she made for me and used it as a pillow to lay down on the floor by her feet, when she sat down for a moment's respite from housework. I felt so secure in her presence.

It was so comforting to have her hands rub Cloverine or Rosebud salve on my frequently sustained *boo-boo's*. "Kiss it" was not a request, nor offered. Just that she was there was enough.

Occasionally, someone gave us a newspaper.

"Read the funny papers to me," I begged to Mother. I was fascinated by the antics of the Katzenjammer Kids, the cherubic appearance of Dolly Dingle, the Toonerville Trolley.

"Tell me a story," I would say to her, at which she was extraordinaire. She did so to entice me to take a nap or at bedtime, before my nighttime prayer. She was there all day long.

I can see her now, where she often sat between household chores at the treadle sewing machine, positioned under a window for maximum lighting. There she stitched baby clothes, patched worn thin garments, or mended seams.

With the school day ending at 4:00 P.M. in the 1930's-1940's, after-school snacks were not options for students who rode a bus. It was suppertime when we got home; Mother would be putting it on the table. Always there!

At the end of the day, there was no hesitancy or fear about going to bed. I had had a hot and filling meal, and I knew that when I awakened Mother would be there.

She guided me through adolescence, puberty, and a first date that went awry, saying: "That happened to me once too." Always there.

Fond memories of bonding with my dad come from the long walks on Cleveland Road, that we used to take in the evening. Many opportunities arose to experience this togetherness. Our footsteps made not a sound on the smooth, hard-packed surface of the dirt road. Even though the rocks and trees sometimes took on an eerie appearance, and I imagined all sorts of apparitions reaching out from the shadows, I never was afraid in the company of my dad.

When the sharp silhouettes of the trees became deepening forms, finally indistinguishable at all, nocturnal wildlife emerged. The air filled with sounds. In early spring the shrill crescendo of pollywogs, interspersed occasionally with the mating croaks of mature bullfrogs, dominated.

Whip-poor-will, whip-poor-will or *Who-who-whoo-whoo-whoo!* might sound in the distance. Once, a mournful wail pierced the air. Startled, I lunged toward Dad causing him to sway off balance.

"What?" he exclaimed. Interrupting him, I babbled out what I had heard.

"Screech Owl," he replied, remembering the call from his youth when his hearing was normal. Where the name came from was a mystery. It sounded nothing like a screech to me. Dad smiled at my bewildered reaction as we moved on. Gradual loss of hearing for my dad was not as devastating to him as one might think. He no longer had to fake it that he didn't hear Mother's request for needed household repair, and it made for memorable quality-time spent together for him and me.

Continuing with the holidays: my family was busy with tourists on the Fourth of July. The only way we celebrated as kids was to wave some lighted sparklers in the air. Once after closing the Inn, we did attend a fireworks display over the water in Schroon Lake, New York.

Labor Day was notable only because the new school year started shortly thereafter. It was never considered a holiday, as we attended to daily chores and the tourists.

Halloween was limited to spooky tracings in school art class and ghostly stories in books. If Trick or Treating were a custom in town, my brothers 'nor I never knew about it.

Other than Christmas, Thanksgiving was the most important holiday for us. Fall harvest was taken care of. The busy tourist and hunting seasons had ended; we could even afford some store-bought candy and nuts. A sense of quiet in the cool, autumn air matched the cozy warmth of the woodstoves in the house. With aromas of a big meal cooking, and children and pets running around, there was a feeling of thankfulness that all was right in our own little world, at least for the day.

Christmas, in light of what was being celebrated, merits a special discourse. I learned that at a young age. At the farm, many memories of Christmas seasons gone by came alive for me, the first one beginning with the tree at the store. This was where it had come from.

I had watched Mother hang the big ornaments and twisted glass icicles, about four inches in length, on the branches. Both had been inherited from my great-great-grandparents, she mentioned. The colorful balls, hand-painted with designs, were tissue-paper thin, packed and unpacked ever so carefully each year. In their fragility, they and the icicles were the only decorations on the tree.

I was too young for that wild anticipation of Santa's visit, but I knew without a doubt that only some magical, mystical figure could have left an orange in my stocking, and a new pair of shoes for me the previous year. There were no exotic toys for children of my generation, certainly no media to expose us to whatever could be purchased.

"But I wanted a wiggle-doll," I sobbed the year the church Santa gave me a stiff boy doll with painted hair. No one knew what I meant until the following year, when Mother had figured it out. That year Santa left a homemade rag doll, with rows of stitching across the arms and legs where joints would have been. The appendages did wiggle, and I loved that doll. My belief in Santa Claus was strengthened.

Most memorable was the year that I fell over the child's wicker rocker to reach the wicker doll carriage behind it.

"How did Santa know I wanted a doll carriage?" I uttered in disbelief.

"Probably grandpa and grandma told him," Mother answered. She must have felt a momentary pang of disappointment that I had overlooked the chair in favor of the carriage. She had spent many, long hours selling products from the Larkin Soap Order catalog to her neighbors to earn the chair as a premium.

Grade school fueled my imagination of a childhood Santa Claus. Each classroom had a Christmas tree brought in by a student. We decorated them with construction-paper chains, and later cornucopias made in a higher grade. Some of these, brought home, filled in the spaces of our own tree, left empty by the inevitable breakage of the fragile, old Christmas ornaments. Students drew names from a hat for an exchange of presents, a tradition to this day among members of some large families. Friday afternoon assemblies emphasized the Christmas story of Jesus' birth. That this action would ever become an issue of church versus state was unimaginable.

With knowledge of St. Nicholas and customs of the Old World, my excitement for the Holiday peaked. When older and wiser (?) students *pooh-poohed* the belief in Santa Claus, I resolved that those were the kind of kids who found a lump of coal in their stocking Christmas morning. Still, it did raise doubts about him. Who was this plump, little man with a jelly-belly, always portrayed wearing a red suit?

I was up so early that Christmas morning Mother was forced to light the kerosene lamps. He did come! All doubts concerning his reality were temporarily dismissed when I found a piece of clothing not handmade or school supplies I didn't know existed under the tree. Santa had even filled some of the cornucopias with delicious hard Christmas candies.

He certainly knew how to add sparkle to the sparsely-decorated tree. Colorful birds, with real feathers and spun glass tails, perched here and there on branches where shimmering, foil icicles hung down.

I never thought about my parents forming many friendships with city travelers who frequented the Adirondacks and our Inn at the time that might have remembered me at Christmas.

Even as I aged and realized the myth, Christmas morning was somewhat spectacular as Mother always held out a couple of nicer gifts, putting them under the tree after everyone else was in bed.

Fast forwarding to high school: decorations made by elementary students covered the huge tree set up in the gymnasium. We often traded names we drew to get someone's name whom we had a crush on. A Christmas program by the music department featured many of the age-old religious carols we still love today. Santa Claus was out of the picture completely, or was he? My interest in the holiday became more self-centered. Who would want my name? Would anyone?

One year I used a remnant of flannel material from one of Mother's sewing projects to make a scarf for a boy whom I hoped would notice me. He wasn't impressed. Another time, the extra gift of an Eversharp fountain pen and pencil set from a young man was the thrill of my lifetime to date. It was the significance of the friendship ring today.

I will always remember my first Christmas away from home after graduating from high school. It was when I was boarding at my great-Uncle Burke Cross's home in Connecticut. He received a call from the railroad station depot that something needed to be picked up from the freight yard. Dad had sent a Christmas tree wrapped in burlap. Nestled among the branches was a bird's nest (an ancient omen of good luck) and several groups of cones—a touch of my Adirondack home.

My parents were equally surprised to find a very-heavy parcel by their mailbox that year. I had sent them some new batteries for the radio I had given them a few years before. Mother wrote of the joy felt from receiving the surprise package adding: "But your father had to hitch up the horse and sleigh and go all the way around the roads to get it home."

Although my last Christmas at home before entering the work world was the most memorable, it was one of the saddest.

It was the year Mother died of a sudden heart-attack on December 16, 1944. Somehow family had gotten through the funeral. As the only girl in the family, still in my teens, I was left to comfort Dad and felt I should make Christmas dinner for married brother's families. Like Humpty Dumpty my life was shattered, never to be whole again. How was I ever going to manage?

My reverie was broken by a knock on the door, interrupting the deafening silence that morning.

"I didn't know until this morning. Maybe this is something you can use," great-Uncle Ludwick Turner, standing there and holding out a wrinkled paper bag, said to me.

My arms sagged with the weight. Although he had walked for miles from his home to ours, no amount of persuasion could convince him to come in and get warm.

"No, no, got to get home before dark," he remarked, turning away. His roundtrip would take all day.

Opening the bag, I found a roasting pan containing a turkey, stuffed and cooked, plus a jar of gravy alongside. This would be the first, and only, turkey dinner my family ever had. Mother would have been so happy. It must have been Uncle Luddie's own Christmas dinner given to him by some charitable organization.

Yes indeed, there was a Santa Claus. He didn't have to be chubby with a bulging belly and full white beard, recognized immediately by the red suit he wore. He could be a humble, shabbily-dressed little person with a big heart.

*D*uring the war, a work rule existed that a person, who was exempt from military service due to being employed in a job important to the war effort, mustn't change jobs. Max, a truck driver for Barton's garnet mines, did not think this applied to work that was equally important. When an opportunity arose for a millwright position with National Lead Company, he took it. He was immediately inducted into the Armed Forces. He was 35-years-old. It was a blessing in disguise that Mother had not lived to see this happen. But thanks to

Maxwell during a moment of relaxation with the U.S. Army.

the Serviceman's Readjustment Act (known as the GI Bill) of

1944, by the 1950's he had a truck of his own and a successful trucking business in North Creek, where he and his family lived.

Verne and his family had a home on Route 28, opposite the Cleveland Road entrance/exit, and like Dad, worked in the woods. The time he had spent in conservation projects with the CCC served him well in that field.

Ernie, I, and our two daughters were living in our basement while building a home overhead, in the "suburbs" of North Creek. He was back at work with National Lead Company and I (by choice) was a stay-at-home mom and loving it; "just a housewife" like my mother, until the *nest was empty*.

My dad held very few nine to five jobs, none of which he applied for. He saw no reason to commit to a regimented lifestyle, and was convinced that the only noble way to make an honest living was by self-employment off the land. He believed that by the way he lived, others should be aware of his work skills and seek him out for help. I differed with his opinion, when I learned in high school English class how to write a letter of application for a job.

My birth certificate listed him as a mechanic, perhaps because he had been employed on the Indian Lake highway for a boss, named John Rust. I do remember him in a substitute position of sanding main roads in wintertime for James Fagan, the Town Superintendent of Highways.

He liked to work with horses, and spoke of handling a horse and wagon in one of the area garnet mines when he was younger. In the same capacity, he did haying at Thirteenth Lake Lodge, and other places on Christian Hill, and North River village. He also drove a team of horses used to clear the land, for the railroad tracks into the National Lead Company mines. But all these jobs were temporary.

As a widower, living only with his dog, Doc, he now worked the deteriorating farm alone. Electricity was still not available in that area, but there was a commode in the house that I had helped him acquire when Mother was ill. He had been commissioned by Milford Benton, County Superintendent of Highways, to keep Cleveland Road passable by removing debris after a storm, and to keep ditches clean so rainwater could run freely thereby avoiding a washout.

Over 60-years-old, he no longer tracked deer over hill and dale, or placed hunters on watches as he had always done, but he enjoyed watching the animals feeding under the ancient apple trees nearly every evening. In a day to come, he was to catch sight of a lone hunter crossing the field—not an unusual sight as many did so to get to state land beyond, where it was excellent hunting territory. Posting No Trespassing signs was never considered those days. Only a greenhorn would tarry in someone's back yard.

By the showy, hunting clothes the person wore, and the hesitancy of his walk, Dad recognized him as one of those greenhorns, so watched him carefully. Sure enough, the stranger took up a stance at the corner of the barn, some 50 feet from the house.

"What da' ya' think y're doing here?" Dad asked, quickly approaching the intruder.

"This looks like a good place to watch," the man stammered, mouth agape at seeing someone come from a place that appeared to be abandoned.

"It's a damn good place to watch, and I'm watching it!" Dad answered, with the wry humor of only an Adirondacker—adding "If 'ya know what's good fer' 'ya, ya'll make fast tracks out 'a here. THIS IS PRIVATE PROPERTY!"

Conclusion

Although it appears that deprivation was a way of life during Prohibition, the Great Depression, and World War II, we did not see it that way. We did not miss what we never expected to have. Every day was just a challenge to be dealt with as we lived, made a living, and looked forward hopefully to the next one—just everyday folks.

Made in the USA
Lexington, KY
28 September 2015